Theodore Roosevelt National Park Planning Guide

Kenneth Perry

Kenneth Perry

Copyright © 2021 ALL RIGHTS RESERVED.

Written by Kenneth Perry
Reviewed by Cindy Perry
Edited by Tiffany N. O'Brien
Photographs by Kenneth Perry unless credited otherwise.

No part of this book may be reproduced or transmitted in any form by any means, electronic or mechanical, including photocopying and recording, or by any information storage and retrieval system, except as may be expressly permitted in writing from NationalParkPlanningGuidesInfo@gmail.com.

ISBN-10: - 1-946490-37-7
ISBN-13: - 978-1-946490-37-7

DEDICATION

I would like to dedicate this collection of planning guides to two important people in my life: my son, Joe Perry, for revitalizing me with a desire to search out and enjoy this beautiful country and its natural resources and explore all of the National Parks; and my lovely wife, Cindy Perry, who has supported me in the writing of this planning guide. I am very fortunate to find a special woman that not only enjoys nature, travel, etc., but is always up for the next adventure that I come up with.

CONTENTS

	Dedication	i
1	How to use the planning guide	1
2	Overview	3
	ADA Accessibility	4
	RV Restrictions	11
	Park Visitation	11
	Historical Temperature and Rainfall	12
3	History	13
	Geological History	13
	Cultural History	14
	People of the Area	14
	Park History	15
	Park History Timeline	16
4	Activities	17
	National Park Scheduled Events	17
	Backcountry Camping	24
	Bicycles	24
	Canoeing/Kayaking	25
	Cross country skiing/Snowshoeing	25
	Golfing South Unit	25
	Golfing North Unit	26
	Horseback Riding	26
	Hiking with Pets	26
	Fort Union Trading Post National Historic Site	33
	Misouri-Yellowstone Confluence Interpretive Center and Fort Buford State Historic Site	37

	Knife River Indian Village National Historic Site	38
	Lewis Clark Interpretive Center and Fort Mandan State Historic Site	39
5	Personal Favorites	41
	South Unit Personal Favorites	41
	Scenic Drive	41
	Geological Features	42
	Short Hikes	43
	Wildlife Viewing	47
	Photography	49
	Activities in Medora	50
	North Unit Personal Favorites	55
	Scenic Drive	55
	Geological Features	55
	Short Hikes	57
	Wildlife Viewing	58
	Photography	59
	Elkhorn Ranch	60
6	Accommodations	62
	Backcountry Camping	62
	Camping the South Unit of the park	62
	Camping the North Unit of the park	64
	Camping at Elkhorn Ranch in the park	64
	Camping near the South Unit	65
	Camping near the North Unit	66
	Camping near Fort Union/Fort Buford/ Confluence Interpretive Center	66

	Hotels near the South Unit	68
	Hotels near the North Unit	70
7	Restaurants	73
	South Unit - Medora, ND and Dickinson, ND	73
	North Unit - Wadford City, ND, Williston, ND, and Sidney MT	74
8	Transportation	81
	Transportation near the South Unit - Billings, MT and Bismarck, ND	81
	Bismark, ND - Bismark Airport (BIS)	81
	Billings, MT - Billings Logan International Airport (BIL)	82
	Transportation North Unit	83
	Williston, ND - Amtrak (WTN) and car rental	83
	Williston, ND - Sloulin Field International Airport (XWA)	83
9	Other Government Units	84
10	National Park Planning Guides	86
11	About the Author	88

1 HOW TO USE THE PLANNING GUIDE

The National Park Planning Guide is a collection of the most current information to help plan a "great adventure". The book is designed to eliminate hours of research for all the things you need to consider when planning your vacation. Instead it puts all of the information in an organized and easy-to-use format to help you plan your vacation.

This book will provide:

- Overview - Basic park information and unique park specific items like Park Shuttles
- ADA Accessibility - Within the park.
- History - Briefly talk about people, culture, geology etc.
- Accommodations - Detailed Lodging and Campgrounds inside and outside the park
- Booking Tips - When to book accommodations, tours, etc.
- Activities - Inside and outside of the park
- Restaurants - Inside and outside of the park, listed by type of food
- Other Government Parks in the area
- Also included National and State Parks Units - Fort Union Trading Post National Historic Site, Knife River National Historic Site, Ft Buford State Historic Site, and Missouri-Yellowstone Confluence Interpretive Center

This planning guide is available in both eBook (downloadable to your iPhone, Android, iPad, tablet, or laptop) and paperback.

Make sure that you visit our website: NationalParkPlanningGuides.com for additional high level planning information and more, such as:

- Blog with RSS feed - All of the latest information on the planning guides
- Photos - Please feel free to copy and use any of the photos that are on the website
- Online Store - find your books easily on Amazon with direct links to purchase the books
- Revisions - Updated information
- Planning Information - Includes historical temperature/rainfall/accommodations/comprehensive activities matrix for all National Parks
- Book Releases - Includes both current and books planned to be

- released within the year
- Comments - Leave a comment and/or register for notifications of book updates and releases

Even though I am focusing my eBooks and paperback books on the 62 National Parks, there is so much more that the National Park Service provides for us to visit and explore. These include:

National Battlefields (11)
National Battlefields Parks (4)
National Battlefields Site (1)
National Military Parks (9)
National Historic Parks (58)
National Historic Sites (76)
International Historic Sites (1)
National Lakeshores (3)
National Memorials (31)
National Monuments (85)
National Parks (62)
National Parkways (4)
National Preserves (19)
National Reserves (2)
National Recreation Areas (18)
National Rivers (5)
National Wild and Scenic Rivers and Riverways (10)
National Scenic Trails (3)
National Seashores (10)
Other Designations (11)

Total of 423 National Park Service units as of January 11, 2021

Thank you and have a great adventure…

2 OVERVIEW

Theodore Roosevelt was not always a National Park. In 1935 the Roosevelt Recreation Demonstration Area was created, and in 1946 it became the Theodore Roosevelt National Wildlife Refuge under the United States Fish and Wildlife Service. In 1947 it became the Theodore Roosevelt National Memorial Park. In 1978 Congress established Theodore Roosevelt as a National Park. The park covers approximately 70,448 acres, located in the northwestern part of North Dakota, and was visited by 691,658 people in 2019.

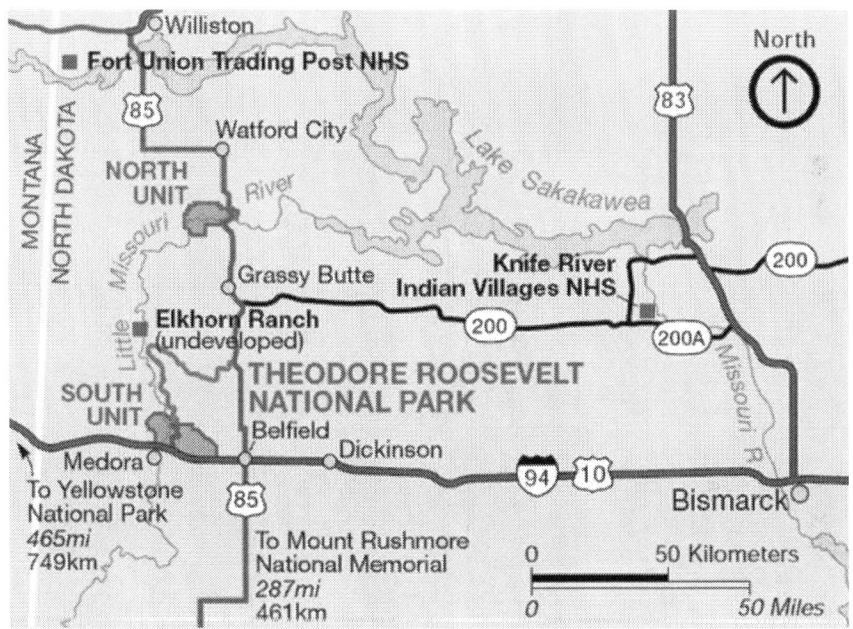

North Dakota National Parks:Area Map

Contact Information: 315 Second Avenue, Medora, ND 58645

Website: https://www.nps.gov/thro/index.htm

Mailing Address: PO Box 7 Medora, ND 58645

Phone number: (701) 623-4466

GPS Coordinates:

South Unit entrance: N46°54'57.6" W103°31'35.9"
North Unit entrance: N47°35'59.4" W103°15'37.1"
Elk Ranch entrance: N47°14'21.5" W103°37'29.4"
Painted Canyon: N46°53'42.5" W 103°22'54.1"

ADA Accessibility
All three park visitor centers are wheelchair accessible, as is the Maltese Cross Cabin. Park films shown at the North and South Unit visitor centers offer closed captioning. Link to a list of ADA compliant facilities: https://www.nps.gov/thro/planyourvisit/accessibility.htm
Source: NPS

List of ADA accessible areas:

Nature Trails and paths
- The short trails at the Skyline Vista Overlook and Boicourt Overlook in the South Unit
- Little Mo Nature Trail in the North Unit are hard surfaced with minimal slope. All other trails have unmaintained dirt surfaces.

South Unit Areas
- Skyline Vista - 0.1-mile trail
- River Woodland Overlook - sidewalk with view of the Little Missouri River
- Prairie Dog Town near the loop road junction - sidewalk and exhibits
- Scoria Point Overlook - sidewalk, exhibit, and viewing area
- Badlands Overlook - sidewalk, exhibit, and viewing area
- Buck Hill - sidewalk and exhibit (trail is paved and gravel with stairs)
- Beef Corral Prairie Dog Town - sidewalk with prairie dog viewing
- Wind Canyon Trail Parking Area - sidewalk only; trail is dirt and gravel surfaced with stairs
- Boicourt Overlook - sidewalk and exhibit

North Unit Areas
- Longhorn Steer Pullout - sidewalk and exhibit
- Slump Block pullout - sidewalk and exhibit
- Cannonball Concretion pullout - sidewalk, exhibit, and cannonball concretion viewing

- River Bend Overlook - compacted gravel trail to viewing deck and exhibit
- Oxbow Overlook - paved path along the rim of the badlands, exhibits

Campgrounds
- The South Unit's Cottonwood Campground has four accessible campsites and two restrooms that meet ADA access requirements.
- The South Unit's Roundup Horse Camp also has accessible toilets and a picnic pavilion.
- The North Unit's Juniper Campground has two accessible sites and two restrooms meeting ADA requirements. The group campsite also has accessible restrooms.

Admission Fee: 7-day pass prices: $30 for non-commercial vehicles, $15 for Bicycles, $25 for Motorcycles.

If you have a 4th grader in your family, a special FREE pass is available for the entire family. Go to this website for more information. www.everykidinapark.gov

Hours: Open every day, 24 hours a day, 365 days a year. However, the visitor centers have reduced hours and dates of operation from September through June.

Pet Information: Pets are permitted with some restrictions (https://www.nps.gov/thro/planyourvisit/pets.htm). Pets must be kept on a six-foot leash. They are allowed only in developed areas which include: campgrounds, picnic areas, parking lots, and on the roadways. They are not permitted on trails and in the back country.

As always, please clean up after your pet.

Passport Stamp Locations: https://www.eparks.com/documents/cancellations.pdf

There are 6 stamps for this park: Medora, South Unit, North Unit, Painted Canyon, Watford City, and Elkhorn Ranch. The Elkhorn Ranch stamp is ONLY Available at Medora Visitor Center upon request.

Visitor Centers/Museums/Sites:

- **South Unit Visitor Center -** Information, park movie, park passes, exhibits, historic cabin, and Theodore Roosevelt Nature and History Association Bookstore. On display is the shirt that Theodore Roosevelt was wearing in a failed assassination attempt.

- **North Unit Contact Station -** This is a small Visitor Center with a gift shop, park information, and park movie (available upon request at the front desk). Its not uncommon to see some of the large Buffalo just outside of the contact station.

- **Painted Canyon Visitor Center -** Panoramic views, hiking trails, information, and Theodore Roosevelt Nature and History Association Bookstore. The parking lot is shared as a "rest area". In addition to the great views, allow some time to take a hike into the canyon below.

- **Elkhorn Ranch -** There are several interpretive signs along the way and at the site. From the parking area it is a short hike to the ranch which borders the Little Missouri River. You can see the foundations of the buildings. This is the site where Theodore Roosevelt spent much of his time while in North Dakota. When visiting from the South Unit, if you would rather drive on paved road more than dirt roads, I would recommend using paved road ND16 and turn right on Black Tail Road, then follow the instructions for visiting from the north. Instructions are in the park brochure.

Campgrounds

- **Cottonwood Campground (South Unit) –** Seasonal; fills to capacity mid-May through mid-September (approximately 50 percent can be reserved at https://www.recreation.gov). See the activities chapter for RV and Big Rig site numbers.

- **Juniper Campground (North Unit) –** Seasonal; fills to capacity mid-May through mid-September. Sites at Juniper are first come, first served. See the activities chapter for RV and Big Rig site numbers.

- **Roundup Group Horse Camp (South Unit) -** Seasonal

- **Petrified Forest** - Located on the western part of the South Unit. Access off of I94 and through hiking trails. Explained in the hiking section.

Safety, Safety, Safety…

Our National Parks are some of the most beautiful places on earth. Many have inherent dangers where we can lose our life if we're not following the recommendations of the park service and also using good common sense. Even with all of the warnings from the National Park Service, needless loss of life occurs every year. In 2020 a teenage girl could have lost her life when she decided to walk between two large male bison that were reported fighting earlier (during mating season is when they are the most unpredictable). One male bison charged and gored her leg and threw her in the air. Luckily, there were other visitors that saw the attack and summoned help. She was air-lifted to the hospital in Bismarck. The needless attack could have been prevented, so please do not let this happen to you!

ENJOY, but be safe.

There are no lodges or hotels in Theodore Roosevelt National Park. There are two campgrounds and one equestrian camping area inside the park boundaries.

Overview of the National Park and Theodore Roosevelt
The public has been trying to protect the North Dakota Badlands since the early 1900s. Work by the Civilian Conservation Corps began in 1934 and continued through 1941. They completed projects in what would become the North and South Units. The park was opened in 1935 as the Roosevelt Recreation Demonstration Area. In 1946 it became the Theodore Roosevelt National Wildlife Refuge under the United States Fish and Wildlife Service. Then in 1947 it became the Theodore Roosevelt National Memorial Park. In 1978, it became the Theodore Roosevelt National Park in honor of Theodore Roosevelt, the 26th President of the United States.

Theodore Roosevelt was born in 1858. He loved to be out in nature, hunting and fishing. In 1883 he came to the Badlands of North Dakota and fell in love with the area. He first invested in a local ranch called the Maltese Cross. Later, he started his second ranch known as the Elkhorn Ranch, where he went into business with two acquaintances who managed the ranch. He did go back to Washington DC, but his true love was back in the rugged west of North Dakota. During his time spent in North Dakota is when he realized over-hunting and over-grazing of the land would exhaust our natural resources. Theodore Roosevelt is the only president to significantly set aside land to protect and conserve our natural resources for future generations to enjoy.

During his time in office, he established:

150 National Forests (created the United States Forest Service)

51 Federal Bird Reserves, now managed by the United States Fish and Wildlife Service (USFWS)

4 National Game Preserves

5 National Parks (created under the Department of Interior)

- 1902 Crater Lake National Park, OR
- 1903 Wind Cave National Park, SD
- 1904 Sullys Hill, ND (now managed by US Fish and Wildlife Service)
- 1906 Platt National Park, OK (now part of the Chickasaw National Recreation Area)
- 1906 Mesa Verde National Park, CO

18 National Monuments

- 1906 Devils Tower, WY
- 1906 El Morro, NM
- 1906 Montezuma Castle, AZ
- 1907 Chaco Canyon, NM
- 1907 Chalmette Monument and Grounds, LA (now part of Jean Lafitte National Historical Park)
- 1907 Cinder Cone, CA (now part of Lassen Volcanic National Park)
- 1907 Gilla Cliff Dwellings, NM
- 1907 Tonto, AZ
- 1908 Muir Woods, CA
- 1908 Grand Canyon, AZ (now a National Park)
- 1908 Pinnacles, CA (now a National Park)

- 1908 Jewel Cave, SD
- 1908 Natural Bridges, UT
- 1908 Lewis & Clark Caverns, MT (now a Montana State Park)
- 1908 Tumacacori, AZ
- 1908 Wheeler, CO (now Wheeler Geologic Area, part of Rio Grande National Forest)
- 1909 Mount Olympus, WA (now Olympic National Park)

Theodore Roosevelt National Park has lots to explore…

There are two major sections of the park to explore, the South and North Units. The South Unit includes the Painted Canyon and the Petrified Forest; both units offer very different terrains and habitat. The North Unit is probably your best chance of seeing wildlife. The North and South Units are about two hours apart, but it is well worth the trip to visit both of them. While in the South Unit, plan to explore the Painted Canyon trails and visitor center. To visit the Painted Canyon, take Exit 32 on I-94 and follow the signs. Between the North and South Units is the area where Theodore Roosevelt built his second ranch, the Elkhorn Ranch.

Birdwatching

Theodore Roosevelt is a great place for birdwatching. The park has over 185 different species that frequent the park throughout the year. Here is the checklist broken down by the four seasons:
https://www.nps.gov/thro/learn/nature/upload/Bird%20Checklist.pdf
At Elkhorn Ranch, birds appeared to be louder. Without the noise of cars and visitors, there you will really be able to appreciate the peace and enjoyment that Theodore Roosevelt probably felt while at his ranch beside the Little Missouri River.

Mammals

The only animals that are easy to spot in the park are the bison, black-tailed prairie dogs, and feral horses. Others, like the big horn sheep, deer, and elk are more difficult to spot and can be found more often in the North Unit. Your best opportunity to spot wildlife is near sunrise or sunset.

Astronomy and Night Sky Viewing
Light pollution is low in the park, offering an amazing view of the heavens. The Dakota Nights Astronomy Festival historically has been held near the end of August/early September.

Handy Links

    Web cameras: https://www.nps.gov/thro/learn/photosmultimedia/webcams.htm
    Campground Maps: https://www.nps.gov/thro/planyourvisit/camping.htm
    Equestrian Maps: https://www.nps.gov/thro/planyourvisit/horseback-riding.htm

Equestrian Camping is offered at Theodore Roosevelt National Park; see this website for additional information:
https://www.nps.gov/thro/planyourvisit/horseback-riding.htm

RV Restrictions on park roads

The are no restrictions for recreational vehicles (RVs) and trailers on any of the roads. "However, there are sections of the road which are very narrow, have sharp curves, and/or have steep grades. As such, operators of these vehicles must exercise caution while driving in the park. You are sharing the road with other motorists, bicyclists, pedestrians, and wildlife." Source: NPS

Park Visitation

When do most visitors visit Theodore Roosevelt National Park? This will give you a good overview of the attendance based on monthly totals for 2019.

Jan	Feb	Mar	Apr	May	Jun	Jul	Aug	Sep	Oct	Nov	Dec
3 K	2 K	9 K	17 K	84 K	132 K	176 K	138 K	103 K	63 K	16 K	4 K

Source: NationalParkPlanningGuides.com

122 Historical Temperature and Rainfall

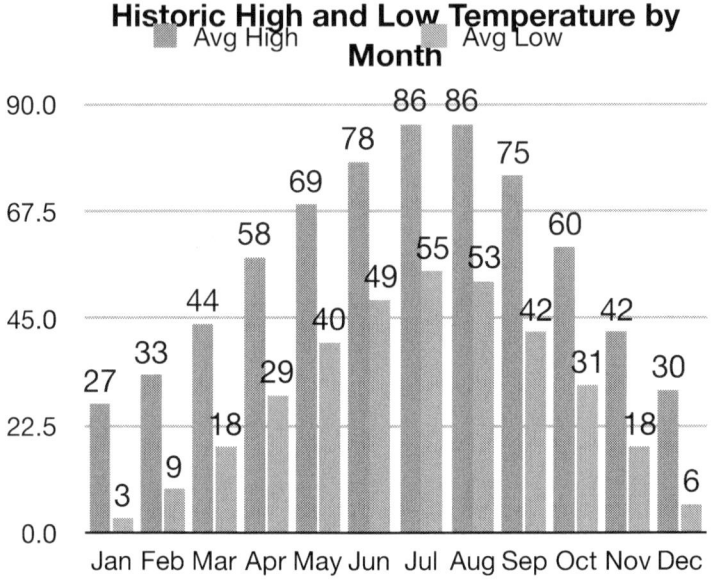

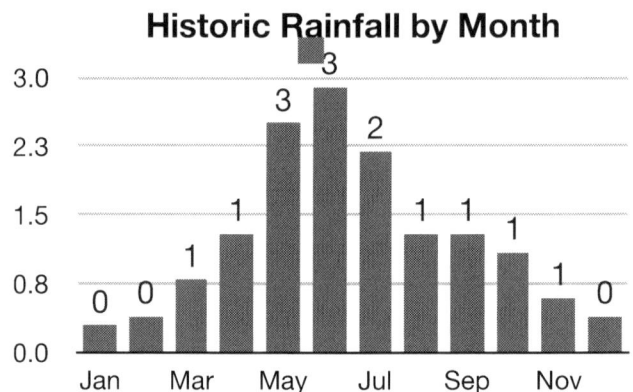

3 HISTORY

Geological History

Interesting geological features exist throughout Theodore Roosevelt National Park and can be seen along your journey. See the "Personal Favorite Chapter" for locations of amazing features.
The earth and the environment have always been in a state of change. Scientists say between 55 and 60 million years ago, this area was once a thriving, arid tropical environment with flourishing plant, animal, and small crustaceans, much like Florida.

Geological Features at Theodore Roosevelt

Fort Union Formation - Explorer Ferdianad Hayden in the early 1800s identified the first fossil of the Fort Union Formation when he found a fresh-water fossil. The formation became known as the Fort Union Formation. This fossil is now on display in the Smithsonian Museum in Washington, DC. The Fort Union Formation is sandstone, shale, and coal beds. The coal beds are some of the largest coal reserves in the United States. The formation extends north into Canada and south into Montana, Wyoming, and North Dakota.

Glacier Erratics (North Unit) - During the Pleistocene Ice Age (from 2.6 million to 11,700 years ago) there were repeated glaciations. The glacier movement over the earth's surface caused abrasion and the plucking of rocks as it carved the mountainous terrain. Larger sheets of ice carrying large rocks, known as erratics, were deposited on the terrain and appeared as the sheets of ice started to melt. Erratics can be identified by looking for rocks different from others in the area based on their composition.
Slumping (North Unit)- Slumping is caused by erosion of the lower levels of the earth's surface. Probably the best example is at the first pullout on the right in the North Unit.

Cannonballs (North Unit) - The correct name is 'concretions', but they are sometimes referred to as cannonballs. Cannonballs can be found at the Cannonball pullout (approximately 5 miles from the Visitor Center). The best cannonballs are not on the trail that you are tempted to take but back around the corner to the right. The cannonballs were formed over millions of years first from a grain of sand. Inside, you can see the layers of sediment which contributed in the making of the concretions.
Petrified Trees (South Unit) - Petrified trees can be found in many areas of

the park. They are easy to spot since they look kind of like a tree but are hard and more like a rock. Like the erratics, they do not match any of the other rock features nearby.

Bentonite (Both Units) - Bentonite is a blueish-gray clay created from volcanic ash. When you see it up close on a trail it looks like popcorn. You will usually see them near the top of a plateau. When wet, the Bentonite is slippery and hiking becomes near impossible.

Coal Veins (Both Units) - Coal veins can be found throughout the park. They are easily identified by black horizontal layers in the formation. Coal fires can result from manmade fires or those touched off by nature through lightning. The fires can burn for many years before they burn themselves out. As the fires burn the ground above will collapse, leaving a crater looking area. The best example of coal veins is at the North Unit as you head north upon exiting the park. Also, the Coal Vein Nature Trail in the South Unit is well worth the short hike.

Cultural History
As with most National Parks in the west, presence of various American Indian tribes was found visiting the area as far back as 7,500 years ago. Tribes that visited this region include the Arikara, Assiniboine, Blackfeet, Chippewa, Cree, Crow, Gros Ventre, Hidatsa, Mandan, and Sioux. During that time, the American Indians lived off of the land, and most of these tribes were nomadic, traveling with the season and food sources. Buffalo was the major animal hunted as it provided not only food, but also clothing, blankets, tipi coverings, tools, toys, decorations, and other uses.
Civilian Conservation Corps (CCC) - The Civilian Conservation Corps was created by President Franklin D. Roosevelt during the 'Great Depression', 1933 to 1945. The CCC provided work for many young men across the country. The CCC built structures and trails to improve the park infrastructure. The CCC began building structures, trails, and campgrounds in 1934 even before it was even a National Park Unit. Approximately 600 men in three companies completed projects in both the North and South Units. In the North Unit they built two picnic shelters: Juniper campground, and the River Bend Overlook shelter, which is still used today. In addition, they built some of the park roads and developed trails. The CCC Campground is managed by the United States Forestry Service.

People of the Area

Marquis de Mores - Marquis de Mores, a French Nobleman, established the town of Medora, named after his wife Medora Von Hoffman. Her father was a wealthy Wall Street banker. Marquis plans were to become one the largest (approximately 3,840 square miles) cattle rancher in North Dakota. Marquise also establish a meat processing plant to provide beef to the east coast at a lower cost. The endeavor was a disaster and the meatpacking plant closed by 1886. After two bad years of drought and bitter cold winters, losing most of his herd, they eventually moved back east.

Theodore Roosevelt - In 1883, Roosevelt left his pregnant wife and departed on a train to the west to hunt bison. Not knowing anyone, he launched out on an adventure which changed his whole outlook through the course of his life.

With the Northern Pacific Railroad cattle could be transported back east, easily making ranching an attractive business opportunity, and with the stroke of a pen, he purchased the Maltese Cross Ranch for $14,000 ($355,643 in today's dollars) in 1883. In 1884, he purchased his second ranch, the Elkhorn Ranch about 35 miles north of Medora. Theodore Roosevelt wrote several books while in North Dakota, one entitled Hunting Trips of a Ranchman, written in 1885 and told cattle herds were diminishing due to overgrazing. This observation was the foundation which drove him as president to set aside land to protect the natural resources then and for future generations. It was in 1886-1887 that the harshest weather hit the Badlands of North Dakota. Most ranchers lost 80 percent of their herds due to the lack of feed (the land had been overgrazed). Even though Theodore Roosevelt only lost fifty percent of his herd, he sold off the Maltese Cross Ranch to his partners to minimize his loses.

Harold Schafer - Harold Schafer started his career in Bismarck, North Dakota. He started a company called the "Gold Seal Company" making floor wax which was not profitable. In 1945 he introduced Glass Wax and by 1948 it went national. Then he developed Snowy Bleach and finally his most well known product in the 60s, Mr. Bubble Bubblebath. After selling the business, he reinvested most of his money into the Theodore Roosevelt Medora Foundation. The Schafer's were very generous and helped finance many causes. When visiting the town of Medora, you will see just how loved and missed the Schafer's are.

Park History

I find the park history for Theodore Roosevelt more dynamic than most parks, as many of the parks typically transition from being a National Monument into a National Park. This park, however, it would appear that no one knew what to name it or what category it belonged in. Perhaps, they were trying to pick a name based upon the virtues of the man for which it was named after. No matter what the correct name was called in the past, it became a National Park.

Park History Timeline
- 1934 - 1941 CCC completed projects in what would become the North and South Units.
- 1935 Roosevelt Recreation Demonstration Area was created.
- 1946 The area was renamed "Theodore Roosevelt National Wildlife Refuge" under the United States Fish and Wildlife Service.
- 1947 The area was renamed again to "Theodore Roosevelt National Memorial Park", which was the only memorial park in the NPS system. It included both the South Unit and Elkhorn Ranch Unit.
- 1948 The North Unit was added to the Theodore Roosevelt National Memorial Park.
- 1968 The East Entrance ceased operation and a new entrance, now known as the South Entrance, was opened in the town of Medora off Interstate 94 (I-94).
- 1978 Congress established Theodore Roosevelt as a National Park.

4 ACTIVITIES

National Park Scheduled Events

Every National Park has a Junior Ranger Program. More and more adults are also becoming Junior Rangers, and some sites even have a "Not So Junior Ranger" badge or "Senior Ranger" badge. The information in the program books is top notch. I obtained my first Junior Ranger badge in Yellowstone, and I was not only impressed with the quality of the content (great Overview) but it was fun. I had a Ranger from Theodore Roosevelt National Park visit me while I was working at Fort Union Trading Post National Historic Site and wanted to do the program. After he completed the workbook and obtained his badge, I told him that I was going to visit the South Unit and wanted to get my Junior Ranger badge. We visited the South Unit multiple days and completed all of the hikes and every activity. The Ranger was so impressed, he gave me one of the wooden Junior Ranger badges which were handed out during the 2016 Centennial Anniversary of NPS. Even if you don't compete in the program, I would recommend getting the workbook for the wealth of information it contains.

Calendar of events: https://www.nps.gov/thro/planyourvisit/calendar.htm

Information below is from 2019 programs which were more typical. The Covid-19 pandemic in 2020 greatly reduced most parks offerings.

	Time	Description
Maltese Cross Cabin Tour	30 minutes	Located just outside the South Unit Visitor Center, Roosevelt's cabin provides a glimpse into his experiences ranching in Dakota Territory.
Through the Prairie We Go	1 hour	Join a ranger and other park visitors for a group exploration of one of the park's many hiking trails. Along the way, discuss the natural features and processes you observe. Hikes vary in distance and difficulty.
The Roosevelt Experience Wilderness Hike	3 hours	Join a ranger and other park visitors for a group exploration of one of the park's many hiking trails. Along the way, discuss the natural features and processes you observe. Hikes vary in distance and difficulty.
Bison Chat	1 hour 30 minutes	Find out about our National Mammal and the work the Park is doing to improve the specie's future at the Painted Canyon Overlook (I-94 exit 32)

	Time	Description
Petrified Forest Hike	2 hours	Join a park ranger on a 3-mile hike to the Petrified Forest. Meet at the South Unit Visitor Center at 9:15 a.m. to caravan your vehicles to the trailhead. Bring plenty of water, dress for the weather, and wear sturdy shoes.
Geology Talk	30 minutes	The dramatic, dissected landforms and spectacular vistas of Theodore Roosevelt National Park allow visitors to experience the continuous processes of erosion that have created the rugged landscape of the Little Missouri Badlands.
Little Program on the Prairie	45 minutes	It's not just grass growing in the prairie! Come learn about the diversity of the prairie and what lives hidden in the grasses...or not so hidden.
Searching for Home	45 minutes	Participate in an in-depth discussion on the concept of "home" through the eyes of the Lakota tribe and homesteaders that lived in the badlands. Geared towards adult audiences.
A Big Stick to Perch On	1 hour 30 minutes	Hike an easy, 0.3-mile trail and search for the birds that Theodore Roosevelt loved.
SettlingDown in the Badlands	1 hour	Come see the Badlands as early settlers and American Indians would have; could you have called this place "home"? Meet the ranger at the Little Mo Nature Trail for this easy, 1.5 mile hike.
Committee, Kettle, or Wake?	45 minutes	What do you call a group of turkey vultures feasting on a carcass? Discover these fascinating birds and their unusual (and sometimes gross) habits.
A Minor Setback for a Major Comeback	45 minutes	Come and learn about wild turkeys; one of the most successful conservation stories in our nation's history!
Crucible of Conversation	45 minutes	Learn from a ranger what Theodore Roosevelt can teach us about conservation.
Theodore Roosevelt National Park 101	1 hour 30 minutes	Meander through one of the most popular hikes in the South Unit and learn about many of the fascinating facets of the Park. This is an easy-moderate 0.3 mile hike.
Tiny Universe	45 minutes	A look at the wonderful world of insects.

	Time	Description
The Evolution of the Little Missouri Badlands	1 hour	Learn how the Little Missouri Badlands evolved from 65 million years ago to what you see today. This moderate 0.8 mile hike starts at Coal Vein Trailhead.
Park Pastime	45 minutes	The Civilian Conservation Corps was a 1930s relief program that helped young Americans find work while providing invaluable service to our state and national parks. Discover the past of Theodore Roosevelt National park and how the CCC, along with other federal conservation projects, shaped the park into what it is today.
Megafauna Management	45 minutes	Learn about the park's bison, horses, and elk and how they interact with the landscape, visitors, and each other.
Fire Ecology	45 minutes	Discover the inner-workings of the prairie ecosystem and find out what makes fire such an important ecological factor in the grasslands.
Naturalist Notebook	1 hour 30 minutes	Meet at Talkington Trailhead located between mile markers 17 and 18 for a moderate, 1.5 mile hike exploring prairie plants and wildlife in the spirit of Lewis and Clark.
Sperati Point Vista	1 hour	Join a ranger for 2.4 miles, easy-moderate hike and witness the jaw-dropping views that only the Little Missouri Badlands can provide. Hike starts from Oxbox Overlook.
Cowboys- The Men Behind the Myths	45 minutes	Cowboys and ranchers forged ahead through hardships in the western North Dakota landscape. Come hear about the hard work behind the myths and misconceptions!
Game Trail Gambol	2 hours	Join a ranger for a 1.5 mile hike along some of the park's game trails, and see the park as the wildlife do. This is a strenuous, off-trail hike.
BioBlitz: Night Herping	1 hour 45 minutes	Come join a ranger for one of our BioBlitz events! This event will be focusing on searching for reptiles and amphibians along the park's scenic drive. Participants will need to drive their own vehicle.
Junior Ranger Adventure	1 hour	Complete a Junior Ranger book, hike the trail with a ranger (0.8-mile, easy), and earn a badge! Bring water, dress for the weather, and wear sturdy shoes. Family inclusive program.

	Time	Description
Jr. Ranger Prairie Dog Fun!	1 hour	Learn about the park's "keystone species" and earn your Junior Ranger badge on this two-mile, easy hike. Meet the ranger at Caprock Coulee Trailhead.
The Resilient Spirit of the Nation	45 minutes	Travel in time to see how bison and humans interacted with each other throughout the past, present, and future.

Hiking South Unit

Name	Ability Level	Distance Round Trip	Description
Skyline Vista South Unit	Easy	0.1 mi / 0.16 km	Feel the wind in your hair high atop Johnson's Plateau. This flat, paved nature trail is perfect for those who want to step out for just a moment.
Boicourt Overlook Trail South Unit	Easy	0.2 mi / 0.3 km	One of the most beautiful South Unit overlooks is accessible by this easy nature trail with slight grade. This overlook is a ranger favorite for sunsets over the badlands!
Little Mo Trail North Unit	Easy	0.7 mi / 1.1 km (paved inner loop) 1.1 mi / 1.8 km (unpaved outer loop)	Explore the river bottom habitat along a paved nature trail with slight grades. Take along a trail brochure, available at the trailhead, to learn as you adventure.
Buck Hill South Unit	Easy	0.2 mi / 0.3 km	You'll be on top of the world when you climb to the highest accessible point in the park. This is a short, but steep trail. The view from the top is worth every step.
Wind Canyon Trail South Unit	Easy	0.4 mi / 0.6 km	Enjoy hiking this nature trail alongside a wind-sculpted canyon as you climb to the best view of the Little Missouri River the South Unit has to offer. Another ranger favorite for sunsets!

Name	Ability Level	Distance Round Trip	Description
Ridgeline Trail South Unit	Easy/ Moderate	0.6 mi / 1 km	Explore the badlands environment along a nature trail with moderate to steep grades. Take along a trail brochure, available at the trailhead, to learn as you adventure. This trail has stairs.
Coal Vein Trail South Unit	Easy/ Moderate	0.6 mi / 1 km (inner loop) 0.8 mi / 1.3 km (outer loop)	Although the coal vein is no longer burning, this nature trail is an excellent place to learn about badlands geology and ecology. Take along a trail brochure, available at the trailhead. This trail has stairs.
Painted Canyon Nature Trail South Unit	Easy/ Moderate	0.9 mi / 1.4 km	The canyon looks amazing from the rim, but wait until you experience a hike down into it! Get up close and personal with the rock layers, junipers, and wildlife. Remember, every step down means a step back up on the return.
Maah Daah Hey South Unit	Moderate / Strenuous	7.1 mi / 11.4 km (one way)	The Maah Daah Hey Trail stretches 96 miles across the National Grassland connecting all three units of the park. This portion of the trail runs through the South Unit.
Lone Tree Loop South Unit	Moderate / Strenuous	9.6 mi / 15.4 km	You can begin this trail at Peaceful Valley Ranch by following the Elkhorn Trail. To avoid a river crossing, access the loop via the Maah Daah Hey Trail. This will add 3.2 miles round trip. Be aware of difficult stream crossings.
Petrified Forest Loop South Unit	Moderate / Strenuous	10.3 mi / 16.6 km	Located in the remote northwest corner of the South Unit, this hike takes you through ancient petrified forests and badlands wilderness. The loop includes the North and South Petrified Forest Trails as well as the Maah Daah Hey.

Name	Ability Level	Distance Round Trip	Description
Jones/Lower Talkington/ Lower Paddock Loop South Unit	Moderate / Strenuous	11.4 mi / 18.3 km	This loop combines the Jones Creek Trail, the Lower Talkington Trail, and the Lower Paddock Creek Trail. Add it to the Upper Paddock/Talkington Loop for an epic adventure of 23.4 miles.
Upper Paddock/ Talkington Loop South Unit	Moderate / Strenuous	15.4 mi / 24.8 km 19.4 mi / 31.2 km (Painted Canyon)	This trail combines part of the Lower Talkington Trail with the Upper Talkington and Upper Paddock Creek Trails. Accessing the loop from Painted Canyon will add 4 miles round trip to your hike.

Hiking North Unit

Name	Ability Level	Distance Round Trip	Description
Caprock Coulee Nature Trail North Unit	Easy/ Moderate	1 hour 1.5 mi / 2.4 km	Hike through badlands terrain and dry washes as you experience a variety of habitats. Take along a trail brochure, available at the trailhead, to learn as you adventure.
Prairie Dog Town via the Buckhorn Trail North Unit	Easy/ Moderate	1 hour 1.5 mi / 2.4 km	Start at the Caprock Coulee Trailhead and follow the Buckhorn Trail to a prairie dog town. Be sure to plan some extra time for wildlife viewing; where there are prairie dogs, there are often lots of other animals, too!
Sperati Point via the Achenbach Trail North Unit	Easy/ Moderate	1 hour 1.5 mi / 2.4 km	Begin at Oxbow Overlook. A gently rolling walk leads to an overlook of the Little Missouri River. Along the way, pay attention to the wide variety of forbs and grasses. The prairie ecosystem is one of the most diverse on the planet!
Caprock Coulee North Unit	Moderate / Strenuous	4.3 mi / 6.9 km	The first 0.75 miles of this trail consists of the Caprock Coulee Nature Trail. The trail becomes more strenuous as it climbs to the top of a grassy butte, follows a ridgeline with incredible views, and descends back down.

Name	Ability Level	Distance Round Trip	Description
Buckhorn North Unit	Moderate / Strenuous	11.4 mi / 18.3 km	Hike through prairie dog towns, sagebrush terraces, deep canyons, and high open prairies. Experience the diversity of plant and animal life in these distinct habitats.
Achenbach North Unit	Moderate / Strenuous	18 mi / 30 km	Steep climbs and descents and two river crossings await you on a trail that leads deep into the heart of the Theodore Roosevelt Wilderness. Cross the Little Missouri River at daybreak and climb the buttes to greet the rising sun.

Painted Canyon Unit

Name	Ability Level	Distance Round Trip	Description
Caprock Coulee Nature Trail North Unit	Easy/ Moderate	1 hour 1.5 mi / 2.4 km	Hike through badlands terrain and dry washes as you experience a variety of habitats. Take along a trail brochure, available at the trailhead, to learn as you adventure.
Prairie Dog Town via the Buckhorn Trail North Unit	Easy/ Moderate	1 hour 1.5 mi / 2.4 km	Start at the Caprock Coulee Trailhead and follow the Buckhorn Trail to a prairie dog town. Be sure to plan some extra time for wildlife viewing; where there are prairie dogs, there are often lots of other animals, too!

Source: NPS

Backcountry Camping

Backcountry camping is available year-round at Theodore Roosevelt National Park. The permits are free for a maximum of 14 consecutive days. The main things to know are:

- There is no approved water in the backcountry
- Only commercial fueled stoves can be used
- There are no established campsites

Here is the link to additional information and requirements for planning purposes: https://www.nps.gov/thro/planyourvisit/backcountry-camping.htm

Bicycles

Bicycle usage in Theodore Roosevelt National Park is limited to public roads and is not permitted on any trail.

The good news is there is plenty of mountain biking and hiking with your pet just outside the park on the Maah Daah Hey Trail (MDHT). The trail is approximately 150 miles long, mostly mountain bike and pet friendly on other government lands but not within the National Park (see note below).

Special note from NPS on the Maah Daah Hey Trail: Although bicycling is allowed on the Maah Daah Hey Trail, bicycles are not permitted on that part of the trail passing through the North and South Units of the park.

NOTE: Bicycles cannot be carried or walked over the trail; they must go around the park. Source: NPS

According to the NPS literature, bypassing the North Unit of Theodore Roosevelt National Park can be accomplished by using existing roads. We tried to find alternate roads, but we were not successful… Buffalo Gap Trail is an alternate route that bypasses the South Unit.

Canoeing/Kayaking

"A float trip down the Little Missouri River is an ideal way to experience the beauty and solitude of the North Dakota Badlands. It takes about five days to canoe the 107.5 miles between Medora near the South Unit of Theodore Roosevelt National Park and Long X Bridge on U.S. Highway 85 near the park's North Unit. Two days are needed to continue from Long X Bridge to Lost Bridge on State Highway 22 (Little Missouri Bay on Lake Sakakawea)." Source: NPS

Here is the link for additional information:

https://www.nps.gov/thro/planyourvisit/canoeing-kayaking.htm

Cross country skiing/ Snowshoeing

Winter is the time for visitors and locals to enjoy the peace and tranquility of cross country skiing or snowshoeing the trails. Not all trails will be easily accessible as parts of the park roads may not be plowed in the winter months.

Fishing

If you are thinking about fishing at the park, here is a quote from Theodore Roosevelt

> "Sometimes we vary our diet with fish - wall-eyed pike, ugly slimy catfish, and other uncouth finny things, looking very fit denizens of the mud-choked water..."
>
> Theodore Roosevelt

The park service says that you have a chance get a trophy chub, minnow, blue gill, or carp sucker, but a walleye or pike are only caught on rare occasions.

Golfing South Unit

Medora, ND- I am not a big golfer, however the Bully Pulpit Golf Course is beautiful. The course is truly one with nature and designed to take advantage of the natural badlands landscape.

Medora, ND	Phone	Website
Bully Pulpit Golf Course	701 623-4653	https://medora.com/do/outdoor/bully-pulpit-golf-course/
Medora Mini Golf	701 623-4653	https://medora.com/do/outdoor/new-little-bully-pulpit-mini-golf/

Golfing North Unit

Golfing is available in both Watford City, ND and Williston, ND.

Wadford City, ND	Phone	Website
Fox Hills Golf Course and Country Club	701 842-2074	https://foxhillsgc.com

Williston, ND	Phone	Website
Eagle Ridge Golf Club	701 572-6500	https://www.eagleridgewilliston.com
Williston Municipal Golf Course	701 577-1321	https://www.willistonparks.com/williston-municipal-golf-course

Horseback Riding

There are no longer guided trail rides in Theodore Roosevelt National Park. However, if you have a horse, additional information for horse use and riding in the park is available at: https://www.nps.gov/thro/planyourvisit/horseback-riding.htm

Trail rides are available in Medora which will take you to see the badlands outside the park.

Hiking with Pets

Hiking with pets is not permitted within Theodore National Park on any hiking trail. However, just outside the park boundary are hiking opportunities with your pet.

Hiking with your pets outside the park on the Maah Daah Hey Trail

(MDHT) is permitted. Maah Day Hey was a name given by the Mandan Tribe of North Dakota, which means, "AN AREA THAT WILL BE AROUND FOR A LONG TIME". The trail is approximately 150 miles long, most of which are mountain bike and pet friendly.

Photography

No matter what you like to photograph, you will find it at Theodore Roosevelt National Park. You will find vastly different landscapes between the North and South Units, Painted Canyon, and Elkhorn Ranch. Even different types of wildlife exist between the two parks.

Wildlife Viewing

Wildlife viewing is probably best at the North Unit during the early morning or late evening hours.

Bison (Buffalo) - At the North Unit we saw the most bison at the end of the scenic drive on the big grassy fields. Remember they are wild animals and getting in their personal space (closer than 100 yards) may result in injury or even death. In the South Unit we have seen most wildlife in the back part of the scenic drive.

Prairie Dogs - Prairie Dogs are another common attraction at Theodore Roosevelt National Park. They build large mounds and have a network of tunnels under the ground. The Prairie Dogs form a tight nit community, having sentinels that watch out for intruders and communicates with each other through barking sounds.

Texas Longhorn (North Unit) - Long horn cattle were introduced only in the north unit. They can sometimes be seen on the scenic road between the first pullout on the left to just before the Big Bend Overlook. They spend a significant amount of time in the tree line and down along the river.

Feral Horses (South Unit) - Feral horses are free roaming, once domesticated, horses which are now running wild. Feral Horses can be seen on I-94 near the Painted Canyon and in the South Unit.

Big Horn Sheep (North Unit) - I have not had the fortune of finding the Big Horn Sheep, unlike our visits to Glacier or Badlands National Parks. It seems in Theodore Roosevelt National Park the habitat is different with fewer predators and the taller and rockier terrain makes them difficult to spot. My best suggestion would be to scan the terrain just as you enter the park on the right side. There were Big Horns sightings in 2020 with the construction on the highway at the entrance. A park ranger told me that the construction is disrupting their habitat across the highway where they hang out mostly in the nearby National Forest.

Elk (South Unit) - You are more apt to see elk in the South Unit. There are reports that elk have been spotted closer the entrance near Medora.

Deer - There are both Whitetail and Mule deer at Theodore Roosevelt National Park. Whitetail deer have smaller ears and a brown tail when down and "white'" when raised. The mule deer have large ears (like a mule) and the tail has a black tip.

Pronghorn Antelope - Did you know Pronghorn are the fastest animal in North America and can sustain speeds of 55mph, is the only horned animal that sheds its horns, and the last surviving species of the Antilocapridae family from prehistoric times?

Coyote - May be seen on an early morning or later afternoon hike. We did see plenty of scat on the trails. If you do spot them, they will be off at a distance, mainly in the lower terrain.

Turkey - Merriam wild turkeys can be found at the North Unit in abundance. We saw a number of them at the end of the scenic road.

Rattlesnakes - I listed rattlesnakes not to scare you but to make you aware that they are part of the landscape. Yes, we heard one on our hike to the Petrified Forest west of Medora but never saw him. We also saw one on the Elkhorn Ranch trail, sun-bathing. Most snakes are nonpoisonous; only the Prairie Rattler is poisonous and the good news is that most of the time they will let you know that you are getting close. Usually during the heat of the day, they will not be on the trail but maybe under a bush nearby. In the evening with cooler temperatures, they may come out and lay on the trail or highways to absorb heat from the sand or pavement.

Things outside the South Unit

Medora, ND is a quaint western looking town that started back in 1883 by Marquis De Mores. He named the town after his wife Medora Von Hoffman, daughter of a New York banker.

Marquis De Mores had a vision to move west and create a large cattle ranch and built a meat packing plant to deliver fresh beef back east in his refrigerated railcars faster and a lower cost. Even though he didn't know that he was doomed from the beginning, he found it out quickly. The customers of the beef changed their desire from grass to grain fed beef. And between the drought one year and the harsh winter the following year, his herd was decimated.

Medora Musical - This is probably the most attended attraction in Medora (even with the locals). We attended the performance in August. We booked our tickets in June and were able to get the 5th row center stage. The show changes throughout the season, so even if you have seen it before it will most likely be a different show.

Pitchfork Fondue - It was really hard for me to imagine a pitchfork fondue. My vision was a bunch of stakes skewered on a pitchfork and then cooked over the open fire. Boy was I wrong. See my chapter on personal favorites for the full story.

Carriage Ride - This is a great way to get a nice overview some of the history of the western town of Medora. They provided a list of "must see" things in Medora.

Cowboy Hall of Fame and Indian Museum - There was a short video of introduction to the museum describing the galleries. All of the galleries were well done and focused on topics such as: Native American artifacts and scenes, to the old west cowboy, and rodeo stars.

Chateau De Mores - Before visiting the house, make sure to stop at the Interpretive Center with two large galleries to get properly oriented. The "Hunting Camp" built by the French Nobleman Marquis De Mores. Wait until you visit this "hunting camp". I am sure you will probably walk away with a different vision of the house. This large house was built in 1883 and visited by the wealthy including Theodore Roosevelt. One room of the lower floor was dedicated to preparing for the hunt. This structure is very unique from most which I have visited, since most of the furnishings (approximately 90 percent are original) including an ammunition case with various types of hunting ammunition from the past.

De Mores Meat Packing - Walk around the foundations of the meat packing plant that provided grass fed beef to the east coast in refrigerated rail cars. As part of the area there are several picnic tables, some with shelters, with plenty of parking (even for big rig RVs).

Old Town Hall Theater - There were four shows playing during our visit and we selected "A Teddy Roosevelt Salute to Medora". Joe Wiegand portrayed Theodore Roosevelt and he was absolutely amazing. Joe not only looks like Theodore Roosevelt but sounds like him too. Even though he is telling the story as if he were Theodore Roosevelt, he will break character long enough to reflect current topics and then back to the story without missing a beat. He has made several government performances including a special performance for President George W. Bush at the White House.

Harold Schafer Heritage Center - This is a FREE museum for Harold Schafer on the east side of town. We were so impressed that we wanted to give a donation, but they do not take donations and do not have a donation box. So, who was Harold Schafer? Watch the two videos to understand how Harold and his wife used their wealth from the product creations that he invented to give back to Medora, the town which they loved. One invention I loved most and remember from my childhood was "Mr. Bubble".

Von Hoffman House - The house was built in 1884 by Marquis de Mores for his in-laws and is approximately one mile away from his house. Since the Von Hoffman's lived in Medora, they had to cross the Little Missouri to visit their daughter at the Chateau de Mores located on the hill. Was that by design?

Medora Riding Stables - Located on the east side of town and operates from 7 am to 3 pm. Check out their website at: https://medora.com/do/outdoor/medora-riding-stables-trail-rides/

Transportation Museum - Located on the only road south east of town. Head toward`` the Bully Pulpit Golf Course. Even though you see signs for the Transportation Museum you will never see a building with car, tractors, or trains outside. The museum is actually in the Bully Pulpit pro shop...

Medora Cemetery - Is located at the top of the hill in Medora and is on the right as you climb the hill going to the Medora Musical. There are some old tombstones there. Over by the flagpole is the grave of a man that

De Mores killed in a gun fight. He was acquitted several times. Guess double jeopardy wasn't in the legal system back in those days...

Shopping /Window Shopping

Shop	Phone	Address
Black Hills Gold & Doll Outlet	701 263-5057	362 Pacific Ave
Buffalo Gap Gift Shop and Stitchery	701 623-4393	275 Pacific Avenue
Chasing Horses	701 623-4773	312 Pacific Avenue
Cowboy Lyle's Candy	701 623-4200	265 3rd Avenue
Foxes Den	701 623-3657	358 Pacific Avenue
Hatlee & Brae Ice Cream	701 623-1311	370 Pacific Avenue
Hitching Post	701 623-4488	410 3rd Street
Joe Ferris Store	701 623-4447	251 East Main Street
Made in the USA Mercantile	701 623-4444	251 3rd Avenue
Medora Boot and Western Wear	701 623-1005	200 Pacific Avenue
Medora Convenience Store	701 623-4479	200 Pacific Avenue
ND Embroidery	701 623-1623	394 Pacific Avenue
Roughrider Gift shop	701 623-4444	320 3rd Avenue
Western Edge Books, Artwork, Music	701 623-4345	425 4th Street

Things near the North Unit

Fort Union Trading Post National Historic Site

Website: https://www.nps.gov/fous/index.htm

Phone: 701 572-9083

Facebook: https://www.facebook.com/FortUnionTradingPostNHS/

Instagram: https:/www.instagram.com/fortuniontradingpostnhs/

Fort Union Trading Post was the largest and longest operating trading posts along the Missouri River in the late 1820s owned by John Jacob Astor. The fort traded with the Arikara, Assiniboine's, Blackfeet, Chipawa, Cree, Crow, Hidatsa, Mandan, and Sioux tribes. Fort Union, a Fur Trading Company, owned and operated by the American Fur Company, was built and operated the post from 1828 to 1867. Fort Union traded products from 11+ countries around the world for furs with the American Indians. Approximately 25,000 buffalo robes and other furs were exchanged for trade goods annually.

The fort was reconstructed and completed in 1990s to look just as it was in 1851. It was rebuilt on the original foundations using construction methods and processes used in 1851. Information from an archeological dig, journals, and artist sketches were used to make Fort Union Trading Post historically accurate.

During peak season (Memorial Day through Labor Day), come into the Trade House for a fresh cup of coffee brewed over the open fire just the way it was done in 1851. Talk with a fur trader in period clothing and find out what it was like to work at the American Fur Company post in 1851.

The fort also hosted early explorers heading west, such as George Catlin, Prince MaxiMillion of Wied, artist Karl Bodmer, Father DesMet, John James Audubon, and others. These visitors helped to document with journals and paintings of their manners and customs of most of the tribes. These would become some of the best documented history of the American Indian Tribes in the 1800s.

Special events at the fort are:

Father's Day Weekend - Fur Traders Rendezvous - Fur traders, wearing period clothing, will camp outside the fort that weekend and will provide trade related products for sale, provide demonstrations and living as they did back in the 1800's. The park staff hosts the event and will also be in period clothing with living history demonstrations. Saturday is dedicated for kids with many activities that will hold their interest. There is always plenty to see and do for the adults.

Labor Day Weekend - Living History will bring the fort alive and will be operating as it was in 1851 by both National Park staff and volunteers. Every year is a new program…

Last Bell re-enactment by candlelight - This program is spectacular and it will be a re-enactment of a historical significant occurrence at Fort Union Trading Post. View the fort by candlelight in the way the traders experienced it.

Typically, Saturdays from 10 am to 2 pm are "kids activities" at the fort. Activities are scheduled every Saturday from Memorial Day to Labor Day.

Missouri-Yellowstone Confluence Interpretive Center and Fort Buford State Historic Site

Located about two mile east of Fort Union Trading Post National Historic Site.
Website: https://www.history.nd.gov/historicsites/mycic/index.html
Phone: 701 572-9034
Facebook: https://www.facebook.com/FortBufordMYCIC

Fort Buford and the Missouri-Yellowstone Confluence Interpretive Center are operated by the State Historical Society of North Dakota and are .25 miles apart.

Missouri-Yellowstone Confluence Interpretive Center

The Confluence Interpretive Center offers a great view of the confluence of the Missouri and the Yellowstone Rivers, a nature trail along the Missouri River, two galleries, and gift and bookstore, covered picnic area, and a 20-minute video of Historic Fort Buford "Splendid Isolation".

Fort Buford State Historic Site

Fort Buford was a military fort which was built in 1866 and operated until 1895 at the confluence of the Missouri and Yellowstone Rivers. Take the interpretive tours through one of the actual officer's quarters built in the 1870s and the reconstructed enlisted barracks. Stand in the room where Sitting Bull surrendered in 1881 and visualize what it was like to be stationed in some of the most remote assignments of all military forts. Other areas of the fort are self-guided which include the Officer of the Day building, Guard House which also served as the jail, Powder Magazine, and the cemetery. At the cemetery you will be surprised at how some of the folks actually died…

Special Events at the Confluence and Fort Buford
Paddlefish - Probably one of the strangest fish that I have ever seen. Not only does it look like it came from something in the prehistoric period, it actually did. Paddlefish fishing season starts in early May and ends when the limit has been caught. See ND tourism for more information: https://www.ndtourism.com/articles/paddlefish-season

6th Infantry Re-enactment - A multi-day event of living history with re-enactors, in period clothing, performing some of the day-to-day tasks, including military drills, inspections, and daily life in the infantry.

Knife River Indian Village National Historic Site

Website: https://www.nps.gov/knri/index.htm
Phone: 701 745-3300
Facebook: https://www.facebook.com/KnifeRiverIndianVillagesNHS

This National Historic Site offers many things to see and explore. The Visitor Center and Earthlodge behind the Visitor Center is only the beginning. There is a trail you can take down to the river and see the village that Toussaint Charbonneau and his wife Sacajawea lived in when Lewis and Clark arrived in 1804.

Explore the north part of the site and see one of the largest Hidatsa villages. Then take a hike for some great views of Knife River. Go to the hill where Hidatsa braves would lay in a pit, covered with branches, to catch bald eagles for their feathers with their bare hands.

Special Events at Knife River National Historic Site
Check their website (listed above) for the latest calendar information. Below are listed some of the special events for 2019:

- Pottery Workshop
- Bead Loom Workshop
- Kid's Camp
- Music for the Villages
- Wet Plate Photography / Ambrotype
- Native Language Summit Event

Lewis and Clark Interpretive Center and Fort Mandan State Historic Site

The two sites are less than a mile apart and approximately 20 miles from Knife River Indian Village National Historic Site. A must see for those interested the Lewis and Clark expedition..

Lewis and Clark Interpretive Center

Along with a visitor center, there is a gift shop, and exhibit area. For those following the Lewis and Clark Trail, in this museum you will find the same model of air rifle that Lewis purchased before his journey. Make sure you see the great video that shows the operation and firing the air rifle. The air rifle impressed the tribes, but it was not a very useful or reliable weapon.

Fort Mandan State Historic Site

Take a short stroll to a reconstruction of Fort Mandan, located near where Lewis and Clark built the original one to weather the cold winter cold of 1804. You will be guided through the many rooms appointed with period correct pieces. An interpretive guide will help you visualize how it was back in the winter of 1804. See the small rooms where they lived and worked, preparing for the next part of their journey.

5 PERSONAL FAVORITES

South Unit Personal Favorites

South Unit Print Map

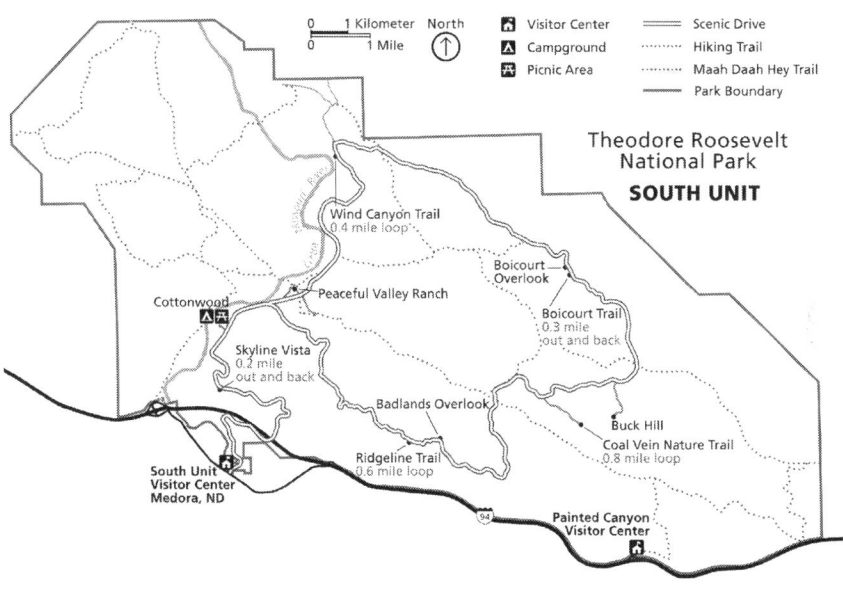

Scenic drive

The Scenic Drive is approximately 36 miles long and takes about an hour and a half to accomplish according to NPS. If you are like me and want to stop and explore, it will be significantly longer.

In 2019 there was a major shift in the terrain in the northeast corner of the scenic drive and a section of the road was closed. In 2020, this section of the road was closed with no prediction of reopening. Currently the part of the road is still accessible by foot, bike, and you can even bring your four legged friend, but no bikes or pets on trails in that area. There was a rumor that the Park Service might re-identify the mile markers to reduce confusion due to future road closures.

Geological Features

Petrified Trees - Petrified trees can be found in a few areas of the park, but you will really have to look for them. They are easy to spot since they look like a tree but are as hard as a rock. The best area to view petrified trees is on the west side of the South Unit. Pick up a map from the visitor center to visit this location.

Bentonite - Bentonite is a blueish gray clay created from volcanic ash. When you see it up close on a trail it looks like popcorn. The Cottonwood Nature Trail near the Cottonwood Campground is one of the best places to see bentonite up close. The nature trail starts from the first little parking lot as you enter the Cottonwood Campground. Park near the small building and walk across the street to join the trailhead.

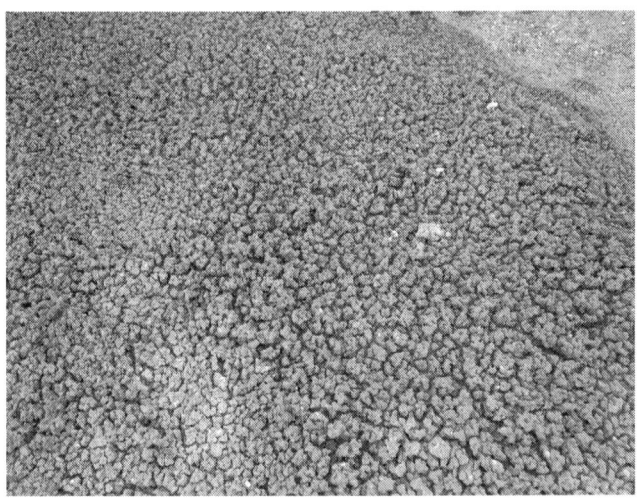

Coal Veins - Coal veins can be found throughout the park. Easily identifiable by black horizontal layers in the formation of rocks. They can be seen on both the South and North Unit Scenic Drives. The best and largest view of coal veins are on highway 85 North of the North Unit entrance. In the South Unit, I would highly recommend hiking the Coal Vein Nature Trail.

Short Hikes

We did all of the short hikes and have provided the recommended hikes below. All but one trail was very enjoyable. Skyline Vista was a short hike; it is really not a vista anymore due to manmade features added to what probably was an amazing view. Refer to the activities chapter, hiking section for details and distances for each hike.

> **Badlands Overlook** - ★★★☆☆ - This pullout offers a nice view but not the best badlands view on the scenic drive and is ADA accessible.

> **Buck Hill** - ★★★★★ - If you thought that Badlands Overlook was impressive wait till you see this view. There is a large circular parking area. The first part is steep, but at the top of the hill you will see the most amazing view of the Badlands. Continue on the trail a short distance to another overlook and vantage point.

Coal Vein Nature Trail - ★★★★★ - Even though it does not show it as a nature hike in the park brochure, when we arrived there it was not only a super nature trail but was guided by one of the park volunteers (Heather). This trail had an information pamphlet at the entrance, but I recommend you download and/or print your own to ensure that you have one. This short trail has sixteen stops. Each stop talks about various aspects of geology. One of the biggest under-ground coal fires burned from 1951 to 1977 (26 years) in this area.

Ridgeline Nature Trail - We almost made it to this trail... With the road closure on the scenic loop road, we decided to take our mountain bikes to the trail. We found out the only way to get there was to start from the prairie dog town when doing the scenic drive counter-clockwise. It had some pretty good up-hill climbs and some beautiful scenery too. We biked 3.4 miles but had to turn around in time to make our previously scheduled trail ride back in town. We will definitely do this next time...

Old East Entrance - ★★★★★ - What a treasure hike this was. Not only is it an historic hike but you get to travel though an impressive Prairie Dog community. After leaving the prairie dogs, you proceed onto a beautifully constructed visitor entrance station that operated in the mid-1940s until Interstate Highway 94 was completed. The new entrance became the South Unit Entrance Station in Medora. The Old East stone structure looks great and is hard to tell that it has been abandoned for many years.

Boicourt Trail - ★★★★★ - This was a really nice trail down to a picturesque overlook. I read an information board and it said if you see smoke or fire call park headquarters. About half-way on the hike what did I see? You guessed it, smoke coming from the ground across the canyon floor. Made a call to report the smoke, then a law enforcement ranger came out and identified it as a coal vein fire.

Skyline Vista - ★☆☆☆☆ - The vista is nothing more than a great view of I-94, the service road to Medora, the town of Medora, a cell tower, and some oil equipment. The only sign for Skyline Vista is when traveling up from the visitor center; we accidentally found this vista on the way out of the park because we did not see a sign. I had a bad feeling about what the view would be like when I drove into the parking lot.
A law enforcement ranger that I worked with at Fort Union NHS told me that "back in the day it really was a scenic view".

Wind Canyon Trail - ★★★★★ - This is a very unique part of the park. The mountains in this canyon were sculpted by wind and rain erosion. The mountain looks to be more similar to sand dunes. The trail takes you to a vantage point of probably the best view of the Little Missouri River in the park.

Petrified Forest - ★★★★★ - A little off the beaten path but well worth the effort. The petrified forest is located on the southwest part of the South Unit. The trail is narrow and the markers are sometimes hard to see; however when you arrive at the petrified trees, the trail opens up and you are able to go out and explore the area.

Wildlife Viewing

Wildlife viewing is great at Theodore Roosevelt National Park but can be unpredictable during the day. During our visits we saw lots of prairie dogs, feral horses, herds of bison, and a few whitetail and mule deer. The best times for wildlife viewing, of course, is early morning and before sunset. The only animal that I know I am going to see is the Prairie Dog at any of the several Prairie Dog Towns.

Bison - One day we were in the park later in the afternoon and saw both feral horses and bison at a distance as well as a few birds and one pronghorn. The next day we did a full morning of hiking and started our hike to the Old East Entrance. On our way back, we saw feral horses up close to the road, and the bison were next to the road. As we started to exit out of the park we came upon a "bison jam".

Horses - Feral horses can be found pretty much anywhere in the South Unit. Sometimes you will see them and bison grazing together along I-94.

Deer - Whitetail and mule deer are best viewed near dusk near the

edge of trees by the Prairie Dog Towns and near the visitor center.

Elk - Elk are best viewed near dusk near the edge of trees by the Prairie Dog Towns and near the town of Medora.

Prairie Dogs - There are several prairie dog towns in the South Unit several along the road, but my favorite is the one on the short hike to the Old East Entrance. If you want to spot other animals, plan to spend some time there and watch for other animals (Coyotes) along the edge that might be looking for a quick meal.

Photography

No matter what you like to photograph, it is probably here in the South Unit. I love to photograph animals, landscape, interesting shapes, etc., while my wife loves to photograph flowers. Here are some of my favorite areas for photographs:

- The Painted Canyon Overlook
- The Ridgeline Trail overlook of the Badlands
- Hoodoos (little towers of earth that have been eroded away by wind and rain)
- Petrified Trees
- Geological features
- Feral Horses
- Bison and Prairie Dogs
- Just to name a few...

Activities in Medora

Medora, ND is a quaint western looking town that started back in 1838. The town was created when a French aristocrat, Marquis de Mores, became one of the largest cattle ranchers in the area.

Medora Musical - ★★★★★ - This is probably the most attended attraction in Medora, even with the locals. We attended the performance in August. We booked our tickets in June and were able to get the 5th row from center stage and were at the same height as the stage. The show changes throughout the season, so even if you have seen it before it will most likely be a different show. I got a tip from a previous guest that while they were waiting for the show; they saw a heard of elk grazing on the hillside.

Pitchfork Fondue - ★★★★☆ - The steaks were arranged on long 'pitchforks' and dipped into kettles filled with oil and boy do they cook fast. I would recommend getting there at least 15 minutes early to grab a seat. There was entertainment and a really good meal overall.

***Note:** They strive to provide medium cooked steaks. There were several hundred at the cookout and we were all sitting down within one half hour. After supper, be sure to walk around the hill-top for some amazing photos of the town below.

Wagon Ride - ★★★★★ - The 30-minute ride starts on 3rd Street and takes you around town. Our guides not only showed us the sites around town but also provided the history from the early beginnings through today.

Cowboy Hall of Fame and Indian Museum - ★★★★☆ - The 20-minute video starts from the beginning of the history of the horse. Did you know that prehistoric horses existed but went extinct? It wasn't until the Spanish introduced horses into our country in the 1500s. Originally horses were found only in the south; however, with trading which existed amongst the tribes horses were found throughout the United States. There are several galleries including Native American, Old Cowboy Life, modern Rodeo, and loads of saddles.

Billings County Court House Museum - ★★★☆☆ - The museum is not that large, however, it is packed with artifacts from life back in the early 1900s, including military, guns, full collection of barbed wire, a room of old tools including the large block plane used to build Theodore Roosevelts Maltese Cross Cabin at the ranch, and even the old jail. Note: They only take cash.

Old Town Theatre - ★★★★★ - There were four shows playing and we selected "A Teddy Roosevelt Salute to Medora". Joe Wiegand portrayed Theodore Roosevelt and he was absolutely amazing. Joe not only looks like Theodore Roosevelt but sounds like him too. It was an excellent show, and I would highly recommend it.

Harold Schafer Heritage Center - ★★★★★ - This is FREE and we were so impressed with the museum for older folks it's kind of journey of some products that Harold created. I knew that I must be really old since I could identify all of them.

Chateau De Mores - ★★★★★ - Between the interpretive center and visiting the house we spent about 2 hours exploring. Even though the owners only lived in the hunting cabin a short time, a lot of things happened there. The Marquis stated on many occasions that his wife Medora was a better shot and rider than himself. Marquis engaged in a duel where he killed a man... Did you know that he almost had a duel with Theodore Roosevelt?

De Mores Meat Packing - ★★★☆☆ - Walk around the foundations of where the meat packing plant existed and provided grass-fed beef to the east coast in refrigerated rail cars. Previously, cattle were shipped by rail car and slaughtered after arriving in the east coast. This new method of shipping beef was thought to deliver a better product. There is a park with picnic tables where you can relax and enjoy a lunch or snack.

Von Hoffman House -★★★★☆ - Louis A. Von Hoffman was a very wealthy New York banker and the father of Medora De Mores. The 1884 built house is well furnished with period furniture both upstairs and downstairs. FREE.

Transportation Museum - ★★☆☆☆ - This transportation museum is not your typical museum. It is located at the clubhouse of the Bully Pulpit Golf Course. Displayed around the room are storyboards about Theodore Roosevelt and the completion of the Panama Canal. He visited the canal and was pictured in the driver's seat of a large crane. He was also the first president to visit a foreign country. It's not a big exhibit, but I am glad I saw it. I would have given it three stars for my interest in the building of the Panama Canal but feel that the majority of visitors may not be so enamored with the Panama Canal.

Medora Children's Park - ★★★★★ - Open year-round and has a western theme for the kids. It looks like an old western town complete with a stagecoach and train engine. FREE. This playground was built in 2001, and the kids will really enjoy this place to explore and have fun.

Medora Mini Golf - ★★★☆☆ - Located across from the Von Hoffman House is the Medora Miniature Golf. If you are looking for some family fun, you can try a round of miniature golf here.

Bully Pulpit Golf Course - ★★★★★ - It was a beautiful golf course with a beautiful backdrop and amazing landscaping.

North Unit Personal Favorites

North Unit Print Map

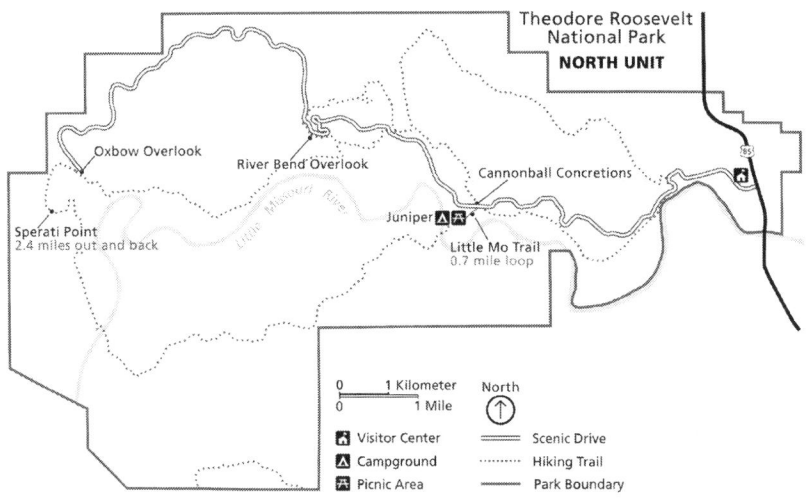

Scenic Drive

If you only have a short amount of time to spend at the North Unit, I would plan to spend at least an hour and a half driving the scenic drive. There are several stops, some with short hikes if you so desire. See the hiking details below for more information. I would recommend stopping at all of the stops, but as a minimum I would stop at the Cannonball Concretions pullout across from the Juniper Campground, the Oxbow Overlook at the end, and the River Bend Overlook.

Geological Features
Fort Union Formation - Explorer and geologist Ferdinand Vandeveer Hayden in the mid-1800s identified a freshwater fossil, which is on display in the Smithsonian Museum in Washington, DC. The Fort Union Formation is made up of sandstone, shale, and coal beds. The coal beds are some of the largest coal reserves in the United States. The formation extends into Canada, to the south in Montana, Wyoming, and North Dakota.

Glacier Erratics - During the Pleistocene Ice Age (from 2.6 million to 11,700 years ago) there were repeated periods of glaciation. As the glaciers moved down from higher ground ripping, abrading, and plucking rocks, it carved the mountainous terrain. Larger sheets of ice carrying large rocks, known as erratics, were deposited on the terrain and appear randomly where they fell off along the way. To identify erratics, look for rocks that are different from others in the area. The erratics at Theodore Roosevelt National Park are much smaller than those I have seen in Glacier National Park and parks in Canada.

Slumping - Slumping is caused by the lower-level rock and debris moves downward on part of the hillside Probably the best example is at one of the pullouts in the North Unit on the right side shortly after you pass the entrance gate.

Concretions - Or cannonballs, as they are known at the park, can be seen at the second pullout on the right which is approximately 5 miles from the visitor center. The trail will lure you in to see a few "cannonballs". For the best "cannonballs" walk around the little hill to the right, approximately 40 yards, and look up in the ravine for some amazing concretions.

Bentonite - Bentonite is a blueish gray clay created from volcanic ash. When you see it up close on a trail it looks like popcorn. You will usually see this from a distance at near the top of a plateau and just about any trail that you hike that takes you near the walls of the mountain.

Coal Veins - Coal veins run throughout the park. They can be identified by black horizontal layers in the formation. Coal fires can result from manmade fires or those touched off by lightning in nature.

Short Hikes
Here are my favorite hikes and are all rated "easy" by the National Park Service…

Some trailheads provide a trail guide to borrow and return but others did not. Lesson learned was to download trail guides to your phone so you know what feature the signposts and markers are showing you. https://www.nps.gov/thro/planyourvisit/hiking-and-trail-information.htm

Little Mo Nature Trail - ★★★★★ - This was a great trail and the short .7 mile loop is ADA accessible, level, and paved for most of it. There are 19 trail markers providing information on berries, trees, geology, CCC projects, and others. After signpost number eight, take the right to what appears to be an animal trail (and I'm sure they use it too). The signposts are all there, however, many of the numbers are not. A very informative hike…

Caprock Coulee - ★★★★★ - Caprock formations are created with a harder rock on top which gets exposed when the lower rock formations are eroded away. The Caprock Coulee and Caprock Coulee Nature Trail listed below form a long one-way trail. We found it easier to park at either end and only hike half of the trail.

Caprock Coulee Nature Trail - ★★★★★ - I would not recommend attempting this trail if there was any rain in the previous 12 hours or multiple days of rain. We had rain the day before and in two spots we almost turned around because of the mud. The trail has 21 information points that are in good repair and easy to find. While on the trail, you get to see some pretty up-close and colorful badlands and some enormous Lignite coal seams flowing down the hill. I also got a shot of a unique caprock that was very thick. I did not get to see the caprock that was on the information board at the beginning of the trail.

Prairie Dog Town via the Buckhorn Trail - ★★★★★ - I hiked it starting at the Cannonball Concretions pullout and from the Caprock Coulee pullout. I would recommend using the Caprock Coulee trail but stay straight to head to the Prairie Dog Town Trail (about 2 miles roundtrip).

Sperati Point via the Achenbach Trail - ★★★★★ - I did this trail as the first hike of the day. Arriving at the visitor Center at 8:30 allowed us to see a herd of mule deer, wild turkeys, and prong horn antelope on our way in. The trail is easy and at the turnaround point, approximately 1.2 miles, we had a great view of the Missouri River and Oxbow feature.

Wildlife Viewing

Most of the animals that we saw in the South Unit are found also in the North Unit. Wildlife was easier to spot in the North Unit and one that can only be found in the North Unit is the Texas Longhorn.

Buffalo- I found the best place to see the large herds of buffalo is at the end of the Scenic Drive where the large grasslands exist. However, be prepared to see them anywhere between the Visitor Center and the turnaround at the end. When you stop at the Visitor Center look close at the ground and you will be able to lots of tracks and even where they rub against the posts.

Prairie Dogs - There are no prairie dog towns which can be seen from the road, but there is a prairie dog town accessible by hiking either the Buckhorn Trail or the Caprock Coulee trail. The shortest hike would be from the Caprock Coulee pullout and is a two-mile, round trip, easy hike.

Turkey - From time to time you may see wild turkeys along the roadside. On one of our hikes, we saw them on the way in and out. Turkeys were spotted on the last third of the Scenic Drive.

Deer - Whitetail and mule deer are best viewed near dusk near the edge of the trees by the Prairie Dog Towns, and near the Visitor Center. Most trails that we hiked had fresh signs of deer and coyote.

Elk - Elk are also best viewed near dusk near the edge of trees by the Prairie Dog Towns.

Bighorn Sheep - Bighorn sheep were never spotted by us, but they tend to hang out in the higher parts of the terrain. We saw a lot of signs posted indicating they are around. In the North Unit they have few predators so you may see them more in the open areas.

Texas Longhorn - The Park Service introduced the Texas Longhorn into the North Unit. A ranger said they sometimes hang out on a grassy plateau where you see buffalo/bison. I also heard from a visitor they saw them in a low-lying area on the left side of the road just past the Visitor Center.

Prong Horn Antelope - We found Prong Horn Antelope were generally found in the last half of the Scenic Drive.

Photography

Landscape - The varied, unique landscape with the vibrant colors. Geological features are all around.
Flora - You will find flowers, berries, and cacti in bloom thriving in the badlands habitat.

Historic - Don't forget the overlook and the beautiful CCC shelter overlooking the Little Missouri River.

Animals - Every trip that I have taken down the Scenic Drive has provided us with some great photos of bison and their calves. I even got a photo of a golden eagle perched above the Little Missouri River, most likely looking for an evening meal.

Painted Canyon Personal Favorites

Badlands Overlook

The Painted Canyon Visitor Center is just north of I-94 at Exit 32. Don't be alarmed that it also appears to be a rest area. The park parking area is at the rear along the canyon wall. The Visitor Center is small but nice with restrooms. The overlook view is better than the Badlands Overlook that is on the Scenic Drive in the South Unit. It reminds me of the overlook at the Grand Canyon but not as vast. If you are visiting this spot around lunchtime, I would recommend bringing a lunch and enjoy the scenery and covered picnic tables.

Hikes

> **Painted Canyon Nature Trail** - ★★★★★ - The trailhead is near the picnic area to the left of the Visitor Center. The park rating of the trail is 'moderate' but was easier than some moderate trails I have been on. There are plenty of stairs on this hike, but I did not find them difficult. When you descend into the canyon, you will walk close to two big peaks that you saw from the vantage point above. If you want to do the minimum number of stairs on the way out of the canyon stay to the left at the sign shows left or straight (which is really to your right). Make sure to bring you camera, as there are some really cool shots at the bottom. If it has rained, do not attempt this hike, as the trail will be very slippery.

Photography
Anywhere around the rim is great for a great picture.

Elkhorn Ranch

The NPS Map and Driving Directions from the north are excellent, however, from the south I would recommend using my directions if you would prefer to spend less time driving on dirt roads.

Here are the GPS coordinates for the Elkhorn ranch. I only use the GPS for situational awareness and identifying streets (I do not follow the guidance).

GPS: N47°14'21.5" W103°37'29.4"

https://www.nps.gov/thro/planyourvisit/elkhorn-ranch-unit.htm

I would highly recommend checking with one of the park units before attempting to visit the Elkhorn Ranch. Road conditions on the entrance road may require 4-wheel and/or a high clearance vehicle to enter. This is the warning that you will receive at the park Visitor Center and it applies to conditions, I assume, after heavy rains. I have taken the road on several trips and found the road to be a normal if not better dirt road i.e., no wash boarding and would not hesitate to drive any car down the road.

From Medora (South Unit) to Elkhorn Ranch I would highly recommend taking the paved road at Exit 1 off I-94 in Beach instead for exit 10 with the NPS instructions. This road has only 18 miles dirt road vs. 40 miles of dirt road following the NPS directions. The drive is a little bit longer but less stressful.

Here are my recommended directions for visiting from the South Unit:

- Take I-94 to Exit 1.
- At the end of the exit ramp, turn right on ND-16 (paved). Follow ND-16 for approximately 29.5 miles.
- Turn right on Black Tail Road/FH 2 (gravel) 12.2 miles.

Now follow the NPS directions as if you were coming from the North Unit.

- Turn right on Bell Lake Road (Still FH 2) for 3 miles.
- Staying on FH 2, turn left towards USFS Elkhorn Campground, 3 miles.
- Continue past campground and MDHT Trailhead to the Elkhorn Ranch Unit parking area.

6 ACCOMMODATIONS

Backcountry Camping

There are plenty of opportunities for backcountry camping a Theodore Roosevelt National Park. Some unique options include winter camping and a boating/camping experience on the Little Missouri. Here is the link for everything you need to know and do for a great backcountry experience. https://www.nps.gov/thro/planyourvisit/backcountry-camping.htm

Camping in the South Unit of the park
Cottonwood is the only campground in the South Unit and has 44 sites. It is dry camping only and no dump station when you leave. See the list of rules for generator use and other items at: https://www.nps.gov/thro/planyourvisit/camping-regulations.htm. Approximately half of the sites are reservable, however, they book up fast. Reservations can be made at: https://www.recreation.gov/camping/campgrounds/251160. The rest of the sites are first come, first serve, so make sure you are the first in line in the morning. Below is a chart that shows the maximum vehicle length for the RV campsites. One anomaly that I have noticed is the way the campground was laid out. Some sites, the door and awning will be on the opposite side of your picnic table location.

Campground	Phone	Website
Cottonwood Campground	877 444-6777	https://www.recreation.gov/camping/campgrounds/251160

Large Site Dimensions

8	Pull Through 40 ft.	9	Pull Through 54 Ft
10	Accessible 41 Ft	12	Pull Through 40 Ft
16	Pull Through 40 ft.	17	Pull Through 77 Ft
18	Pull Through 68 ft.	20	Back In 44 Ft
21	Pull Through 48 ft.	23	Pull Through 50 Ft
27	Pull Through 44 ft.	28	Pull Through 42 Ft
29	Pull Through 46 ft.	31	Pull Through 78 Ft
35	Pull Through 93 ft.	36	Back In 58 Ft
37	Pull Through 75 ft.	38	Pull Through 85 Ft
39	Parallel 40 ft.	43	Parallel 55 Ft
44	Parallel 48 ft.		

Note: Only odd numbers are reservable, even numbers are first come, first serve.

Map of Cottonwood Campground

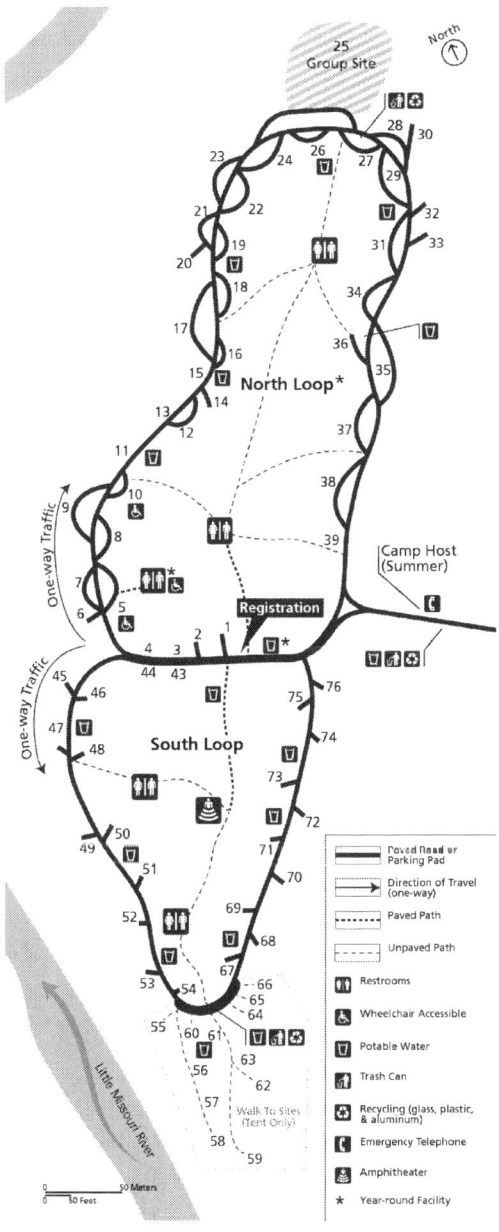

Camping in the North Unit of the park

Juniper is the only campground in the North Unit. It has ~50 campsites and is located on the Little Missouri River. The only campsite that can be reserved is the one Group Campsite. All the others are first come, first serve at the time of this writing

Map of Juniper Campground

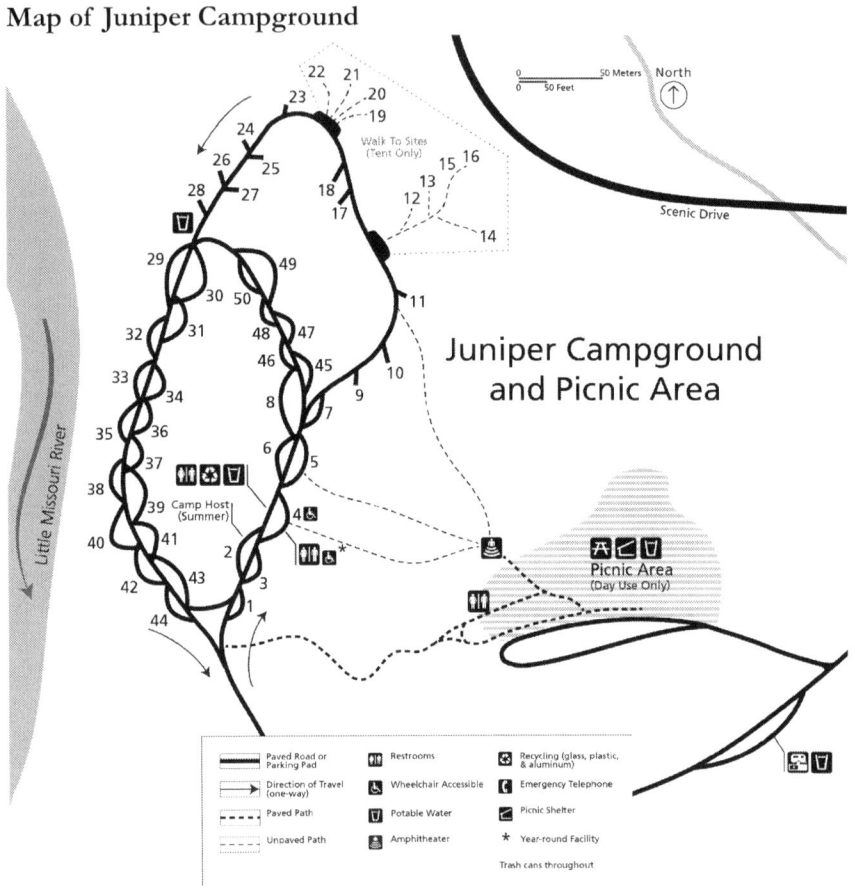

Camping at Elkhorn Ranch in the park

Campground	Phone	Website
Elkhorn Campground	701 842-8500	https://www.fs.usda.gov/recarea/dpg/recarea/?recid=79461

Camping near the South Unit

Camping near the South Unit includes the towns of Medora and Dickinson, ND. Dickinson is approximately 37 miles.

Medora, ND	Amenities	Phone	Website
Medora Campground	WI FH DS PR	701 623-4435	https://medora.com/stay/hotel/medora-campground/
Red Trail Campground	WI FH ST	701 623-4317	http://www.redtrailcampground.com
Bar X Ranch	Equestrian	701 623-4300	http://barxguestranch.com
Sully Creek State Park	DS	701 623-2024	https://www.parkrec.nd.gov/sully-creek-state-park
Roundup Group Horse Camp	Equestrian	701 623-4466	https://www.recreation.gov/camping/campgrounds/251161
Boots Campground	FH	701 260-5180	http://bootsbarmedora.com

Dickinson, ND	Amenities	Phone	Website
North Park Campground	PT, WI, FH	701 227-8498	https://www.campnorthpark.com
Camp on the Heart	FW, DS	701 225-9600	https://thefishergroup.us.com/clients/camp-on-the-heart/
Patterson Lake Recreation Area	FH	701 456-2074	http://dickinsonparks.org/index.php/patterson-lake-recreational-area/

Amenities: BR= Big Rigs, WI= Wifi, PO = Pool, FH= Full Hookups, FS= Free NPS Shuttle, DS = Dump Station, PR= Propane, ST= Store, NH= No hookups, SE= Seasonal Rates, DP= Dog Park, SR= Small RV Only, EL= Electric, PT= Pull Through

Camping near the North Unit

Camping for the North Unit includes campgrounds outside the North Unit and Wadford City, ND. Watford City is approximately 15 miles from the North Unit.

Outside North Unit	Amenities	Phone	Website
CCC Campground	60 ft pads, water	701 842-8500	https://www.fs.usda.gov/recarea/dpg/recarea/?recid=79454
Summit Campground	Tent sites only	701 989-7300	https://www.fs.usda.gov/recarea/dpg/recarea/?recid=79455

Watford City, ND	Amenities	Phone	Website
Arrowhead RV Park	Full	541 206-7816	https://campnative.com/campgrounds/USA/ND/Watford-City/arrowwood-rv-park
Prairie View RV Park	Monthly	701 842-2811	https://www.prairieviewnd.com
Summit Campground		701 989-7300	http://www.fs.usda.gov/recarea/dpg/recarea/?recid=79455

Camping near Fort Union/ Fort Buford/ Confluence Interpretive Center

Camping near Fort Union, Fort Buford and the Confluence Interpretive Center include Buford and Williston, ND and Fairview and Sidney, MT. Distances from Fort Union are:
- Approximately 25 miles to Williston, ND
- Approximately 2 miles to Buford, ND
- Approximately 15 miles to Fairview, ND
- Approximately 25 miles to Sidney ND

Buford, ND	Amenities	Phone	Website
Confluence Interpretive Center	BR NH	701 572-9034	https://www.history.nd.gov/historicsites/mycic/index.html
Confluence Boat Ramp	EL NH	701 577-4500 Beth Innis	https://gf.nd.gov/search/node?keys=camping+Buford

Amenities: BR= Big Rigs, WI= Wifi, PO = Pool, FH= Full Hookups, FS= Free NPS Shuttle, DS = Dump Station, PR= Propane, ST= Store, NH= No hookups, SE= Seasonal Rates, DP= Dog Park, SR= Small RV Only, EL= Electric, PT= Pull Through

Williston, ND	Amenities	Phone	Website
Buffalo Trails	BR WI FH	701 572-3206	https://www.ndtourism.com/williston/campgrounds-rv-parks/buffalo-trails-campground
Williston FoxRun RV		701 334-0579	http://www.willistonfoxrunrvpark.com
Lewis and Clark State Park	FH	701 859-3071	http://www.parkrec.nd.gov/parks/lcsp/lcsp.html
WIlliston Village RV	Monthly only	701 580-2287	http://www.hughesmgt.com/williston-village-rv-resort
BIg Country RV	WI FH	701 609-6429	http://www.bigcountrywilliston.com

Fairview, MT	Amenities	Phone	Website
Fairview Sharbono Park (1)	EL RV	406 742-5616	Overnight parking by the city of. Fairview. Call before 5pm MST
Mindt RV Park	FH	406 489-2669	https://www.facebook.com/firsthaycreek

(1) Sharbono Park is operated by the town of Fairview. Park along curb with easy access to power panels located around the perimeter of the park.

Sidney, MT	Amenities	Phone	Website
RidgeView Park Trenton	Monthly	701 580-1645	http://www.ridgeviewparknd.com/rates.html
Eagle RV Sidney	BR WI FH PT	406 973-7275	http://eaglervparkmt.com
Begnell RV Park	FH	406 480-9119	https://www.facebook.com/pages/category/Sports---Recreation/Bagnell-RV-Park-Campground-336757336854298/

Hotels near the South Unit

Hotels near the South Unit include the towns of Medora and Dickinson, ND.

Medora	Amenities	Phone	Website
Amble Inn		701 623-4345	http://www.ambleinnmedora.com
Badlands Motel	FW FP	701 623-4444	https://medora.com/stay/hotel/badlands-motel/
Cowboy Inn	FW	701 623-4444	https://medora.com/stay/hotel/cowboy-inn/
Dakota Place Lodge	FW	701 623-4444	https://medora.com/stay/hotel/dakota-place-lodge/
Hyde House	FW	701 623-4444	https://medora.com/stay/hotel/hyde-house/
Spirit of the Badlands Lodge	FW FP	701 623-4444	https://medora.com/stay/hotel/spirit-of-the-badlands-lodge/
Wooly Boys Inn	FW	701 623-4444	https://medora.com/stay/hotel/wooly-boys-inn/
Rough Riders Hotel	FW FP	701 623-4444	https://medora.comhttps://medora.com/stay/hotel/rough-riders-hotel/
Eagle Ridge Lodge		701 623-2216	https://www.eagleridgelodge.com

Medora	Amenities	Phone	Website
Elkhorn Quarters	FW	701 623-4444	https://www.eagleridgelodge.com
AmericInn by Wyndam	FB FW FP PO	844 581-4982	https://www.wyndhamhotels.com/americinn/medora-north-dakota/americinn-lodge-and-suites-medora/overview

Amenities: FB = Free Breakfast, FCB = Free Continental Breakfast, FW = Free Wifi, FP = Free Parking, PF = Pet Friendly, PO = Pool

Dickinson	Amenities	Phone	Website
AmericInn by Wyndham	FB, FW	844 388-7316	https://www.wyndhamhotels.com/americinn/dickinson-north-dakota/americinn-hotel-and-suites-dickinson/
Astoria Hotel	FCB, FW, FP, PO	701 456-5000	https://www.stayastoria.com/dickinson-nd
Badlands Inn & Suites	FW, FP, PF	701 225-9510	https://badlandshotel.com
Candlewood Suites	FP, FW, PF, FP	701 761-2050	https://www.ihg.com/candlewood/hotels/us/en/dickinson/
Comfort Inn	FB, FP, FW, PO	701 264-7300	https://www.choicehotels.com/north-dakota/dickinson/comfort-inn-hotels/
Hampton Inn & Suites	FB, FW, FP, PO	701 456-0100	https://www.hilton.com/en/hotels/dikndhx-hampton-suites-dickinson/
Hawthorn Suites by Wyndham	FB, FP, FW, PF PO	701 483-7829	https://www.wyndhamhotels.com/hawthorn-extended-stay/dickinson-north-dakota/hawthorn-suites-by-wyndham-dickinson/
Holiday Inn Express & Suites	FB, FP, PO	701 456-8000	https://www.ihg.com/holidayinnexpress/hotels/us/en/dickinson/
La Quinta Inn & Suites	FB, FP, FW, PF, PO	701 456-2500	https://www.wyndhamhotels.com/laquinta/dickinson-north-dakota/la-quinta-dickinson/

Dickinson	Amenities	Phone	Website
Microtel Inn & Suites by Wyndham	FB, FP, FW. PF, PO,	701 456-2000	https://www.wyndhamhotels.com/microtel/dickinson-north-dakota/microtel-dickinson/overview
My Place Hotel	FP, FW, PF	701 483-0300	https://www.myplacehotels.com/my-place-hotel-dickinson-nd/contact-us
Quality Inn & Suites	FB, FW, FP,	701 456-8400	https://www.choicehotels.com/north-dakota/dickinson/quality-inn-hotels/nd105?destinationEntered=Dickinson
Ramada by Wyndham	FP, FW	701 483-5600	https://www.wyndhamhotels.com/ramada
Red Roof Inn & suites	FB, FW, PF	701 483-1688	https://www.redroof.com/property/nd/dickinson/RRI319
Rodeway Inn	FP, FW, PF	701 227-1215	https://www.choicehotels.com/north-dakota/dickinson/rodeway-inn-hotels/
Roosevelt Grand Dakota Hotel	FB, FP, FW, PF, PO	701 483-5600	https://www.bestwestern.com/en_US/book/hotel-rooms.35041
TownePlace Suites by Marriott	FB, FP, FW, PF	701 483-4724	https://www.marriott.com/hotels/travel/dikts-towneplace-suites-dickinson/

Hotels near the North Unit

Hotels near the North Unit include Wadford City, Williston, and Sidney, ND

Williston, ND	Amenities	Phone	Website
Best Western	FB FW	701 572-8800	https://www.bestwestern.com/en_US/book/hotel-rooms.35038.html
Candlewood Suites	FB PF	701 572-3716	https://www.ihg.com/candlewood/hotels/us/en/williston/wilcw/hoteldetail?
El Rancho	AS FW	701 572-6321	https://www.elranchowilliston.com

Williston, ND	Amenities	Phone	Website
Hampton Inn & Suites	FB FW FP PO	701 774-5909	https://www.hilton.com/en/hotels/isnnrhx-hampton-suites-williston/?
Hawthorne Suites	FB FW FP PF	701 352-6613	https://www.wyndhamhotels.com/hawthorn-extended-stay/williston-north-dakota/hawthorn-suites-by-wyndham-williston/overview?
Holiday Express	FB FW FP PF	701 577-0400	https://www.ihg.com/holidayinnexpress/hotels/us/en/williston/isnwi/hoteldetail?
Landmark Suites	FB FW	701 774-8020	https://landmarksuiteswilliston.com
MainStay	FB FW	701 850-8074	https://www.choicehotels.com/north-dakota/williston/mainstay-hotels
Microtel Inn $ Suites	FB PF	701 577-4900	https://www.wyndhamhotels.com/microtel/williston-north-dakota/microtel-williston/overview?
Motel 6	FW PF	701 774-8152	https://www.motel6.com/en/motels.nd.williston.4648.html
Quality Inn	FB FW FP	701 203-4291	https://www.choicehotels.com/north-dakota/williston/quality-inn-hotels
Ramada	FB FW FP PF	701 609-5555	https://www.wyndhamhotels.com/hotels/williston-north-dakota?

Watford City, ND	Amenities	Phone	Website
Comfort Inn & Suites	FB FW FP	701 842-6565	https://www.choicehotels.com/north-dakota/watford-city/comfort-inn-hotels/nd055?
Little Missouri Inn & Suites	FB FW FP PF PO	701 842-6262	https://www.watfordcitymis.com
MainStay Suites	FB FW FP PF	701 566-7664	https://www.choicehotels.com/north-dakota/watford-city/mainstay-hotels/nd069
McKenzie Inn		701 444-3980	https://mckenzieinn.net

Watford City, ND	Amenities	Phone	Website
Roosevelt Inn & Suites	FB FW PO	701 842-3686	http://www.rooseveltinn.com
Teddy's Residential Suites		701 842-6480	https://www.watfordcitytrs.com
The Watford	FCB FW FP	701 842-6800	https://www.thewatford.com
WoodSpring Suites	FW	701 842-3130	https://www.woodspring.com/extended-stay-hotels/locations/north-dakota/watford/woodspring-suites-watford-city?

Sidney, MT	Amenities	Phone	Website
Best Western	FB, FW, PF	406 433-4560	https://www.bestwestern.com/en_US/book/hotel-rooms.27079.html?iata=00171880&ssob=BLBWI0004G&cid=BLBWI0004G:google:gmb:27079
Candlewood Suites	FW	406 482-9692	https://www.ihg.com/candlewood/hotels/us/en/sidney/sdycw/hoteldetail?
Holiday Inn Express	FB, FW, FP, PF	406 433-3200	https://www.ihg.com/holidayinnexpress/hotels/us/en/sidney/sdyex/hoteldetail?
Lone Tree Motor Inn	FW, FP, PF	406 433-4520	http://www.lonetreeinnsidney.us
MainStay Suites	FCB, FW, PF	406 468-1000	https://www.choicehotels.com/montana/sidney/mainstay-hotels/mt095?source=gyxt
Microtel Inn & Suites	FB, FW, FP, PF, PO	406 626-3556	https://www.wyndhamhotels.com/microtel/sidney-montana/microtel-inn-and-suites-sidney/overview?
Richland Inn & Suites	FB, FW	406 433-6400	Not Provided
Windgate by Wyndham	FB, FW, FP	406 205-0510	https://www.wyndhamhotels.com/wingate/sidney-montana/wingate-by-wyndham-sidney/overview?

7 RESTAURANTS

South Unit - Medora, ND and Dickinson, ND

Medora, ND	Type	Phone	Address	Website
Badlands Pizza Parlor	PZ	701 623-4481	301 3rd Ave	https://medora.com/eat/family/badlands-pizza-saloon/
Boots Bar & Grill	GR	701 623-2668	300 Pacific Ave	https://bootsbarmedora.com
Cowboy Cafe	AM	701 623-4343	215 4th St.	https://www.facebook.com/pages/Cowboy-Cafe/149690881731262
Farmhouse Cafe	AM	701 623-3105	314 Pacific Ave	https://www.facebook.com/thefarmhousecafe/
Gospel Brunch	AM		250 3rd Ave	https://medora.com/eat/family/the-medora-gospel-brunch/
Hidden Java	CF	701 623-4700	350 4th St	https://www.facebook.com/HiddenSpringsJava/
Little Missouri Saloon & Dining Room	GR	701 623-4404	440 3rd St.	https://little-missouri-saloon-dining-room.business.site
Maltese Burger	SU		440 3rd St.	https://medora.com/eat/family/maltese-burger/
Pitchfork Steak Foudue	ST	701 623-4444	3422 Chateau Rd	https://medora.com/eat/family/pitchfork-steak-fondue/
Theodore's Dining Room	AM	701 623-4444	301 3rd Ave	https://medora.com/eat/family/theodores-dining-room/

AM = American, BA = Bar, Saloon, Pub or Tavern, BI= Bistro, BK = Bakery, BQ = Barbecue, BR = Breakfast, CA = Cafe, CH = Chinese, GR = Grill, CF = Coffee Espresso, CS = Coffee Shop, IT = Italian, FF = Fast Food, MX = Mexican, SP = Spanish, SE = Seafood, ST = Steakhouse, SU = Sandwich Shop, UP = UP-Scale, VE = Vegan, PZ = Pizza

Dickinson, ND	Type	Phone	Address	Website
Applebee's Grill and Bar	GR	701 227-8573	289 15th St W	https://www.applebees.com/en/menu
Blue 42 Sports Grill & Bar	GR	701 483-2583	36 W Villard St	http://blue42grille.com
Brickhouse Grille	SE, GR,UP	701 483-9900	2 W Villard St	https://www.brickhousegrilleonline.com
Country Kitchen	AM	701 483-9376	528 12th St. W	http://countrykitchenrestaurants.com
Country Rose Cafe	CA	701 483-2211	837 E Villard St	https://www.zomato.com/dickinson-nd/country-rose-cafe-dickinson
Dakota Diner	GR	701 483-9696	2857 194 Business Loop E	https://www.facebook.com/dakotadiner/
El Pericutin	MX	701 483-6800	455 `5th St. W	https://www.zomato.com/dickinson-nd/country-rose-cafe-dickinson
El Sombrero	MX	701 483-5380	505 15th St. W	https://www.zomato.com/dickinson-nd/el-sombrero-dickinson
J D's BBQ	BQ	701 483-2277	789 State Ave.	https://j-ds-bbq.business.site
Jack's	AM	701 225-5905	1406 W Villard St.	https://www.facebook.com/Jacks-Family-Restaurant-Catering-113526785347362/
King Buffet	CH	701 227-8888	1173 3rd Ave. W	http://dickinsonkingbuffet.com
Los Cabos Family Mexican	MX	701 483-1841	583 12th St. W	http://loscabosmexican.net
Perkins Restaurant & Bakery	AM	701 227-3001	188 W Museum Dr.	http://stores.perkinsrestaurants.com
Pizza Ranch	PZ	701 483-0008	2184 2nd Ave. W	https://pizzaranch.com/locations/nd/dickinson/2184-2nd-avenue-west/menu

Dickinson, ND	Type	Phone	Address	Website
Players Sports Bar & Grill	GR	701 483-1733	2050 1st Ave. E	https://playersbar-grill.com
Sakura Japanese Steakhouse & Sushi Bar	JA	701 483-3888	203 14th St. W	https://sakuradickinson.com
Taqueria el Monte Sinal	MX	701 590-5413	71 W Museum Dr.	https://www.facebook.com/TaqueriaelMonteSinai/
The Wurst Shop	GR	701 483-6384	205 14th St, W	https://www.thewurstshopindickinson.com

North Unit - Wadford City ND, Williston ND, and Sidney MT

Wadford City, ND	Type	Phone	Address	Website
American Smoke Wagon BBQ	BQ	701 842-6790	109 6th Ave SE	https://www.bbqrestaurantwatfordcitynd.com
Burgerrito's	AM	701 651-4775	2008 Main St	https://www.facebook.com/watfordcityburgerritos/?fref=ts
Burrito Bros.	MX	701 444-2002	113 Main St S	https://www.facebook.com/burritobrosND/
Caribou Coffee	CF	701 842-2519	113 6th Ave SE	https://locations.cariboucoffee.com/us/nd/watford-city/113-6th-ave
Champs Chicken	FF	701 444-3639	501 6th Ave SE	https://champschicken.com
China Express	CH	701 842-6666	113 6th Ave	http://www.watfordchinaexpress.com
Giotto's	PZ	701 444-4050	700 4th Ave	https://m.facebook.com/GiottosNeighborhoodPizza/
Godfather's Pizza	PZ	701 842-3704	107 8th St SE	http://godfathers.com
Hardee's	FF	701 805-0750	104 9th Ave SE	https://www.hardees.com/

Wadford City, ND	Type	Phone	Address	Website
Hometown Homemade	BK	701 570-7911	104 4th Ave SE	https://www.facebook.com/hometownhomemadeWC/?ref=bookmarks
Island Kitchens	AM	701 444-4285	722 Main St N	http://islandkitchens.com
JL Beers	GR	701 444-2015	101 Main St S	http://www.jlbeers.com
Little Missouri Grille	AM	701 444-6315	601 2nd Ave SW	
Main Street Grind	CS	701 842-4690	112 Main St S	
Metanoia Mind, Body, Spirit	AM	701 444-2335	604 2nd Ave SW	https://www.facebook.com/Metanoiambs/
Outlaws Bar & Grill	GR	701 842-6859	120 Main St S	http://www.outlawsbarngrill.com
Outsiders Bar & Grill	BA	701 842-2693	905 3rd Ave SW	
Pizza Pie on the fly	PZ	701 651-6732	1005 S Main St	http://ppotf.com
Smiling Moose Rocky Mountain Deli	BR	701 444-3354	1005 Main St Suite 104	http://www.smilingmoosedeli.com
Stonehome Brewing Co.	BA	701 444-5000	313 Fox Hills Parkway	http://www.stonehomebrewing.com
Subway	SU	701 842-6966	105 9th Ave SE	https://order.subway.com/en-us/restaurant/59776/menu/
Taco John's	MX	701 842-6505	109 6th Ave SE	https://locations.tacojohns.com/nd/watford-city/109-6th-avenue-se.html
Teddy's Lounge	BA	701 842-6480	113 9th Ave SE	http://www.watfordcitytrs.com
Tokyo Japanese Steakhouse	JA	701 842-3888	105 9 Ave SE	https://www.facebook.com/pages/Tokoyo-Japanese-Steakhouse-Watford/952477014778206

Wadford City, ND	Type	Phone	Address	Website
Tomate Mexican Grill	MX	701 351-8273	722 Main St N #3	http://www.facebook.com/TOMATEMEXICANGRILL
Twist Mexican Food	MX	701 842-3595	404 2nd Ave SW	https://www.facebook.com/twistmexicanfood/

Williston has numerous food listings, but I have only listed the restaurants with ratings of 4.0 or better.

Williston, ND	Type	Phone	Address	Website
3 Amigos Southwest Grill	MX	701 577-7755	1007 Main St Unit A	http://3amigosgrill.com
Basil Sushi Bar & Asian Bistro	JA	701 572-6688	16 E Broadway	http://www.basilwilliston.com
Bone'z Island Kitchen	AM	701 609-5913	413 Main St	https://www.facebook.com/bonezrestaurant/
Cugini Italian Bistro	BI	701 572-0300	313 Main St	https://www.facebook.com/cuginiwilliston/
Culver's	AM	701 713-4411	401 Reiger Dr	http://www.culvers.com/restaurants/williston-nd
Dakota Farms Family Restaurant	AM	701 572-4480	1906 2nd Ave W	http://www.dakotafarmsrestaurant.com
Doc Holliday's Roadhouse	ST	701 609-5331	3901 2nd Ave W	http://www.dochollidaysroadhouse.com
Don Pedro's	MX	701 774-1151	2516 2nd Ave W	http://www.donpedrosfamilymexicanrestaurant.com
Eleven Restaurant and Lounge	BA	701 572-0544	408 1st Ave E	http://www.thewilliston.com

Williston, ND	Type	Phone	Address	Website
Famous Dave's Bar-B-Que	BQ	701 609-5459	1518 14th St W	http://www.famousdaves.com/Williston
Gramma Sharon's	BK	701 572-1412	1501 16th St W	https://www.facebook.com/pages/category/American-Restaurant/Gramma-Sharons-Family-Restaurant-100861699958614/
Grand Buffet	CH	701 572-1888	1505 15th Ave W	https://www.grandbuffetnd.com
Hula Fire Grill	HA	701 713-4488	23 Main St	http://hula-grill.com
Hula Grill redundant?	BQ	701 713-4488	23 Main St	http://www.hula-grill.com
J Dub's Bar 7 Grill	GR	701 774-2062	1002 2nd St W	http://www.facebook.com/J-Dubs-Bar-Grill-147669621938896/
Los Compadres	MX	701 774-1010	216 Main St	https://los-compadres-steak-seafood-grill.business.site
Meg-A-Latte Coffee House	CS	701 774-8873	204 13th St W	http://www.meg-a-latte.com
Outlaws Bar & Grill	GR	701 609-5075	1319 9th Ave NW	http://www.outlawsbarngrill.com
Pita Place	AM	701 774-0949	819 11th St W	http://www.pitapalace.net
QDOBA Mexican Eats	MX	701 572-5210	120 26th St E	https://locations.qdoba.com
Sakura Japanese Steakhouse	JA	701 572-3888	424 32nd Ave W #12	http://www.sakurawilliston.com/menu.php
Smiling Moose Rocky Mountain Deli	SU	701 572-3354	120 26th St E #600	http://www.smilingmoosedeli.com

Williston, ND	Type	Phone	Address	Website
Spicy Mexican Food (Dakota Deli)	MX	701 713-4197	Site, 2605 19th Ave W #101	https://spicymexicanfood.business.site
Subway	SU	701 572-5846	4001 2nd Ave W	https://order.subway.com/en-us/restaurant/39483/menu/
Williston Brewing Company	BA	701 609-5439	1623 2nd Ave W	http://www.willistonbrewing.com

Sidney, MT	Type	Phone	Address	Website
Asian Garden	CH	406 433-1828	115 E Main St.	http://asiangardenmt.com
Domino's Pizza	PZ	406 630-7788	410 N Central Ave.	http://dominos.com
Footers	FF	406 433-7827	616 S Central Ave.	https://footers.webstarts.com
Fu-Hao	CH	406 433-7900	120 S Central Ave	http://www.fuhaosidney.com
Gullivers	PZ	406 433-5175	120 E Main St. Ste. 14	http://gulliverspizza.com/default/landing
Meadowlark Brewing	GR	406 433-2337	117 S Central Ave.	https://meadowlarkbrewing.com
Mucho Si 2	MX	406 433-2212	202 E Main St.	https://www.facebook.com/MuchoSi2Sidney/
Pizza House	PZ	406 433-1971	710 S Central Ave.	https://www.zomato.com/sidney-mt/pizza-house-sidney/menu
Ranger Lounge	BA	406 482-4566	110 A Central Ave.	http://www.clubplanet.com/Venues/89296/Sidney/Ranger-Loung

Sidney, MT	Type	Phone	Address	Website
Rodiron Grill	GR	406 433-3300	520 N Central Ave.	http://rodirongrill.com
Sadie's	AM	406 433-9949	720 10th Ave. SE	https://www.facebook.com/dooner.f/
South 40	AM	406 433-4999	207 2nd Ave. NW	http://www.south40sidney.com
Sunny's Family Restaurant	AM	406 433-1839	102 E Main St.	https://www.facebook.com/Sunnys-Family-Restaurant-111480028891550/
TapHouse Bar & Grill	GR	406 433-4517	900 1/2 S Central Ave.	https://www.facebook.com/TapHouseSidney/
The Depot	PZ	406 433-4650	2102 S Central Ave.	https://www.facebook.com/TheDepotofSidney/
Winners Pub	BA	406 433-4354	207 2nd Ave. NW	https://www.zomato.com/sidney-mt/winners-pub-sidney

8 TRANSPORTATION

If you are planning a visit to the North Unit, then Williston, ND offers the most convenient transportation for both airlines and Amtrak.

If you are planning a visit to the South Unit, Bismarck, ND and Billings, MT have larger airports. Note: There are no Amtrak stations along the I-94 Interstate highway.

It's approximately a two-hour drive between the South and North Units.
Transportation South Unit - Billings, MT and Bismarck, ND

Bismark, ND - Bismark Airport (BIS)
https://www.bismarckairport.com

Airlines

Bismark, ND	Phone	Website
Allegiant	702 505-8888	https://www.allegiantair.com
American Airlines	800 433-7300	http://www.aa.com
Delta	800 221-1212	delta.com
Frontier	801 401-9000	http://www.flyfrontier.com
United	800 241-6522	united.com

Rental Cars

Bismark, ND	Phone	Website
Avis	800 331-1212	avis.com
Enterprise Rent-A-Car	800 736-8222	enterprise.com
Hertz	800 654-3131	hertz.com

Billings, MT - Billings Logan International Airport (BIL)
https://www.flybillings.com

Airlines

Billings, MT	Phone	Website
Alaska Airlines	800 252-7522	https://www.alaskaair.com
American Airlines	800 535-5225	http://www.aa.com
Cape Air	800 227-3247	https://www.capeair.com
Delta	800 221-1212	delta.com
Frontier	801 401-9000	http://www.flyfrontier.com
United	800 241-6522	united.com

Rental Cars

Billings, MT	Phone	Website
Alamo	877 222-9075	alamo.com
Avis	800 331-1212	avis.com
Budget	800 527-0700	budget.com
Dollar	800 800-4000	dollar.com
Enterprise Rent-A-Car	800 736-8222	enterprise.com
Hertz	800 654-3131	hertz.com
National	800 227-7368	nationalcar.com
Thrifty	800 847-4389	thrifty.com

Transportation North Unit

Williston, ND Amtrak (WTN) and Car rental

Empire Builder, Train 7/27, Westbound, scheduled arrival at 11:07 AM
Empire Builder, Train 8/28 Eastbound, scheduled departure at 6:59 PM

Car rentals at Amtrak Car station

Williston, ND	Phone	Website
Avis	800 331-1212	avis.com
National	800 227-7368	nationalcar.com

Williston, ND - Sloulin Field International Airport (XWA)
http://www.flywilliston.net

Airlines

Williston, ND	Phone	Website
Delta	800 221-1212	delta.com
United	800 241-6522	united.com

Rental Cars

Williston, ND	Phone	Website
Avis	800 331-1212	avis.com
Enterprise Rent-A-Car	800 736-8222	enterprise.com
Hertz	800 654-3131	hertz.com

9 OTHER GOVERNMENT UNITS

The chart below provides the distance and driving time estimates for State and Federal Government Units.

	Distance From North Unit	Distance From South Unit	Website
Badlands National Park	321 miles 5hr 5 min	286 miles 4 hr 34 min	https://www.nps.gov/badl/index.htm
CCC Campground National Forest Service	1 mile 1 min	69 miles 1 hr 4 min	https://www.fs.usda.gov/recarea/dpg/recarea/?recid=79454
Confluence Interpretive Center	63 miles 1hr 5 min	132 miles 2 hr 9 min	https://www.history.nd.gov/historicsites/mycic/index.html
Devils Tower National Monument	281 miles 4hr 35 min	229 miles 3 hr 37 min	https://www.nps.gov/deto/index.htm
Fort Union National Historic Site	65 miles 1hr 6 min	134 miles 2 hr 10 min	https://www.nps.gov/fous/index.htm
Glacier National Park	542 miles. 9hr 8 min	569 miles 8 hr 56 min	https://www.nps.gov/glac/index.htm
Jewel Cave National Monument	335 miles. 5hr 10 min	301 miles 4hr 40 min	https://www.nps.gov/jeca/index.htm
Knife River National Historic Site	109 miles 1 hr 51 min	137 miles 1 hr 58 min	https://www.nps.gov/knri/index.htm

	Distance From North Unit	Distance From South Unit	Website
Little Bighorn National Battlefield	323 miles 4hr 51 min	271 miles 3hr 53 min	https://www.nps.gov/libi/index.htm
Mount Rushmore National Memorial	296 miles 4hr 50 min	262 miles 4hr 20 min	https://www.nps.gov/moru/index.htm
Pompey's Pillar National Monument	305 miles 4hr 18 min	253 miles 3hr 20 min	https://www.blm.gov/visit/pompeys-pillar-national-monument
Wind Cave National Park	328 miles 5hr 28 min	294 miles 4hr 58 min	https://www.nps.gov/wica/index.htm
Yellowstone National Park	536 miles 9hr 48 min	484 miles 8hr 50 min	https://www.nps.gov/badl/index.htm

10 NATIONAL PARK PLANNING GUIDES

Other National Park Planning Guides are available at amazon.com. However, if you go to my website at www.nationalparkplanningguides.com and select the "Online Store" tab, then click on any of the book titles the site will take you to amazon.com where you can purchase an eBook or paperback.

Title	State	Edition	Paperback ISBN	eBook ISBN
Grand Canyon and Petrified Forest National Parks Planning Guide	AZ	1st	978-1-946490-24-7	978-1-946490-23-0
Grand Canyon National Park Planning Guide	AZ	1st	978-1-946490-30-8	978-1-946490-29-2
Petrified Forest National Park Planning Guide	AZ	1st	978-1-946490-32-2	978-1-946490-31-5
Joshua Tree National Park Planning Guide	CA	1st	978-1-946490-26-1	978-1-946490-25-4
Redwood National Park Planning Guide	CA	1st	978-1-946490-28-5	978-1-946490-27-8
Dry Tortugas and Biscayne National Parks Planning Guide	FL	2nd	978-1-946490-16-2	978-1-946490-15-5
Glacier National Park Planning Guide	MT	2nd	978-1-946490-34-6	978-1-946490-21-6
Theodore Roosevelt National Park Planning Guide	ND	1st	978-1-946490-37-7	978-1-946490-36-0
Carlsbad Caverns and Guadalupe National Parks Planning Guide	NM, TX	2nd	978-1-946490-20-9	978-1-946490-22-3

Title	State	Edition	Paperback ISBN	eBook ISBN
Badlands and Wind Cave National Parks Planning Guide	SD	2nd	978-1-946490-14-8	978-1-946490-13-1
Zion & Bryce Canyon National Parks Planning Guide	UT	2nd	978-1-946490-18-6	978-1-946490-17-9
Yellowstone National Park Planning Guide	WY, MT, ID	1st	978-1-946490-12-4	978-1-946490-11-7

ABOUT THE AUTHOR

Kenneth Perry and wife Cindy has visited all 50 of the United States, and all but three provinces in Canada. In addition, he has also visited many European countries, the Caribbean, Mexico. As Ken got closer to retirement age, he had a revelation; he had done a lot of traveling, but he had never really explored all the natural beauty and resources here in the United States.

One of Ken's bucket list items was to visit all of the National Parks and National Monuments with his wife, Cindy. Ken has visited 38 National Parks and 33 National Monuments and many of the other NPS units. As of April 2021, there are 62 National Parks and 85 National Monuments. Ken and Cindy will be traveling in their motor home to visit most of the parks, excluding Hawaii, Virgin Islands, Guam, Samoa, and parts of Alaska. Bailey, their dog, has also been quite the little traveler.

With an engineering and management background and extensively planning family vacations and camp outs, Ken decided to use his experience in the development of planning guides.

Ken is Certified Interpretive Guide and has provided interpretive "Red Bus" tours at Glacier National Park, Yellow Bus and the large bus tours at Yellowstone, and an Interpretive Park Ranger at Fort Union Trading Post National Historic Site.

Have a great adventure!
Kenneth Perry

ISBN-10: - 1-946490-37-7
ISBN-13: - 978-1-946490-37-7

Made in the USA
Middletown, DE
07 September 2024